FISHING THE DRY FLY

Dermot Wilson

Fishing the Dry Fly

Illustrations by Charles Jardine

UNWIN HYMAN

London Sydney

Originally published 1957 by Douglas Saunders with MacGibbon & Kee
under the title 'Dry-Fly Beginnings'
Published in 1970 by A & C Black (Publishers) Ltd under the title
'Fishing the Dry Fly'. Second edition, 1981.

Published in this fully revised third edition by Unwin Hyman, 1987

UNWIN HYMAN LIMITED
Denmark House, 37–39 Queen Elizabeth Street,
London SE1 2QB
and
40 Museum Street, London WC1A 1LU

Allen & Unwin Australia Pty Ltd
8 Napier Street, North Sydney, NSW 2060, Australia

Allen & Unwin New Zealand Ltd with the Port Nicholson Press
60 Cambridge Terrace,
Wellington, New Zealand

British Library Cataloguing in Publication Data

Wilson, Dermot
    Fishing the dry fly.——3rd ed.
    1. Trout fishing——Great Britain
    2. Fly fishing
    I. Title
    799.1'755   SH688.G7

ISBN 0-04-440079-9

Set in 11 on 13 point Plantin by Cambridge Photosetting Services
Printed and bound in Great Britain by Biddles Ltd,
Guildford & King's Lynn

To Fergus Wilson

who tactlessly persists in doing
everything better than his
father can

Contents

Photographs

—◆ **Introduction** ◆—

This book about dry-fly fishing is intended mainly for beginners of
all ages, though I hope that experienced dry-fly fishermen may also
find a few things in it to interest them. It is essentially a collection of
facts, and most of it was first published under the title *Dry-Fly
Beginnings* some years ago. Now I have taken the opportunity to
bring all the original facts up to date, and to include others which
have been brought to light by fishermen or scientists since that time.
I have tried to make them a set of simple but useful facts—the facts
that have been most useful to me, anyway—about catching trout on a
dry fly, about the trout and the flies themselves, and about dry-fly
waters of various kinds, particularly the chalk-streams.

Dry-fly fishing, on the chalk streams especially, has often been
described as an art, and sometimes as a cult. People in fishing books
always seem to be 'initiated into the mysteries of the dry fly', so that
all sorts of secret and probably painful rites come to mind and they
may get the idea that acceptance into the brotherhood of the élite can
come to them only at the end of a very long process. If they take up
dry-fly fishing, they may think they will have to pass through long
years of apprenticeship during which they slowly approach Nirvana
until at last, old and grey, they become high priests too late to do
anything except sit on the bank talking about the Latin names of rare
riverside insects.

What a lot of nonsense! Dry-fly fishing takes less time to learn than
most other sports. Trout—let us whisper it softly—are very foolish
creatures. After all, what do you actually do when you catch a trout
on a dry fly from a chalk stream? First you find a feeding fish—who
gives away his presence by making rings on the surface of the water as
he takes floating flies. Then, taking care not to frighten your trout,
you throw over him a bunch of feathers tied onto a hook, which he
engulfs in mistake for another fly. He does this with complete
innocence although sometimes your bunch of feathers looks very

little like a fly at all. Finally you drag a protesting trout into the net and feel very proud of him. Over-simplification? Perhaps it is. But a good many trout are caught almost as simply as this. Where, then, is all the mystery? And where all the art?

Such art and mystery as do exist in dry-fly fishing probably lie in being able to think like a trout. Some fishermen invariably catch many more trout than others, and strangely enough they are not necessarily the ones who are most skilful at casting, playing and landing. But they do always seem to know quite a bit about the ways in which trout live and feed and behave. And they always seem to get twice as much pleasure out of their sport as well. So, in writing this book, I have tried continually to consider the *trout's* point of view.

Part One hurries rather quickly—as I think is right—over the very elementary mechanism of dry-fly fishing. Part Two is far more important, because it sets down some of the available knowledge about trout and flies. Then Part Three puts a little of this knowledge into practice, containing a few pages also on ethical considerations. Finally Part Four rounds off the volume with two practical chapters on tackle and knots.

Chapter 13, the chapter on tackle, perhaps needs a word of explanation. The many recent developments in fishing tackle can be rather bewildering if they are not explained fully. So I have tried to explain them fully. These explanations can hardly help being a trifle technical at times, so I have placed the chapter towards the end of the book to avoid interrupting the very non-technical way in which I hope to have written the remainder of it. One further point to make is that the chapter deals not only with dry-fly tackle, but with all forms of flyfishing tackle. This leads to a rather better understanding of tackle and may also be of some very direct help to readers who do not intend to concentrate exclusively on the dry fly.

I do not believe that I have passed very far beyond the stage of a beginner myself. Has anyone? This book contains no startling revelations to bring each and every trout inevitably to the net. It simply aims to assemble and present the most important and relevant known facts about trout and about flies. Its object, above all else, is to relate dry-fly fishing as closely as possible to the trout's way of life. I hope that in doing so it may be of some small use to people who enjoy dry-fly fishing, or who think they might enjoy it.

Dermot Wilson

Acknowledgements

It would take many pages for me to list the very large number of friends, some sadly no longer with us, who have contributed to my very small knowledge of fishing. But I cannot help mentioning a few of them, those from whom I have probably learned most. I shall always feel privileged to have known them: Charles Ritz, Frank Sawyer, John Ashley-Cooper, Dick Walker, John Goddard, Reg Righyni, Brian Clarke, Charles Jardine and by no means least, Herbert Wellington in the U.S.A. And then of course there are the very long-suffering friends who have helped me most directly with this book.

My heartfelt gratitude, then, is due to the Earl of Rothes, who first encouraged the writing of it; to Ian Hay of the Rod Box, Winchester, who first suggested the idea of this completely revised edition; to Merlin Unwin, the most patient and helpful publisher I have ever worked for; to Margot Jessop and Jackie Kirby who have painfully but tirelessly deciphered my illegible handwriting in order to produce typescripts; to the late Dr. W. E. Frost, who checked my biological facts about trout; and to the many people who have explained to me, as to a child, the technicalities of tackle—including most particularly Julian Mills.

PART ONE

Elementary Steps

One Trout on a Dry Fly

There is only one secret in dry-fly fishing, which is to make an artificial fly float over a trout in such a way that it looks appetizing enough to him to swallow. All the gear that dry-fly fishermen have, and all the actions they go through, are merely intended to achieve this single aim. All their knowledge about insects, and all their different dry-fly patterns, just help to make the fly more appetizing—because the most appetizing fly to a trout is usually the one that looks most like the natural fly he is feeding on at the moment. Dry-fly fishermen are supposed, also, to creep and crawl around the river-bank on their bellies. The only point of this, when it is done—which is not so often as many people think—is to make sure that the trout is still there when the fly gets to him, instead of being frightened into the nearest weed-bed.

Obviously the right place for a dry fly to be is near enough to a hungry trout for him to see it. The rod and line help to get the fly to the right place. In some places trout are nearly always hungry, usually because there is very little food in the water and they have to make the most of whatever they can find. Then they will often come up to any fly they catch sight of. But in most really good trout waters, where there is plenty of food and the fish are bigger and better-fed and much lazier, they tend to feed at the surface only at certain times of the day, when fairly large numbers of natural flies have appeared and are floating on the water.

Then the trout in lakes and reservoirs cruise around close to the surface, gulping down flies and making a little set of rippling rings every time they do so. This set of rings is called a rise. The trout in rivers take up positions near the surface and wait for the current to carry flies over them. They, too, leave rings behind them on the water when they swallow a fly. You should cast your fly in the path of a cruising trout in still water, or a short way upstream of a stationary trout in a river. In the lake the trout will eventually come towards the fly and in the river the fly will eventually come to the trout, so long as it is cast accurately to him from downstream. It should always float towards him quite peacefully and naturally, at the pace of the stream itself.

Suppose, for instance, that you are on a trout-river and you see a trout rising over by the far bank, where two or three king-cups may be growing by the water's edge. He looks as if he is feeding well, since

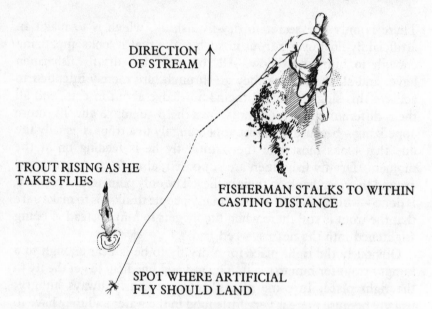

DIRECTION
OF STREAM

TROUT RISING AS HE
TAKES FLIES

FISHERMAN STALKS TO WITHIN
CASTING DISTANCE

SPOT WHERE ARTIFICIAL
FLY SHOULD LAND

every thirty seconds or so the rings of his rise show on the surface as he sucks in a floating insect. The first step of all, usually, is to decide which of your artificial flies is most likely to tempt him. So you have to watch him for a little, to find out what sort of natural insect he is feeding on so eagerly, or at any rate to make a pretty accurate guess. Flies can be seen on the water and several are floating down under the near bank—big, darkish flies with tall, sombre-coloured wings which at king-cup time, in April, can only mean that they are Large Dark Olives. Then, onto your 'cast' or 'leader'—the thin length of nylon which is connected to the end of your line—goes a nicely tied Rough Olive.

Now the fish has to be stalked. This has to be done from downstream, since trout always face upstream. The whole idea is to get close enough to be able to reach him with the fly, yet not so close that you frighten him by your presence or by the waving of the rod. On some heavily-fished rivers trout are notoriously shy and you have to fish for them from a respectful distance; on other rivers they are far more innocent. If you intend to cast from a kneeling position—or if you are wading in the stream—you can probably get rather closer to your trout than if you try to cast standing high up on the bank. Fish feeding well are usually the easiest to approach. A trout who is rising quickly and unhesitatingly, grabbing every fly he can see, is often so concerned with his next mouthful that he will not take much notice of fishermen; a trout rising spasmodically is generally more alert and quicker to take fright.

Sometimes, when you can actually see a trout in clear water, you can tell that he is hungry even if there are no natural flies for him to rise to. A hungry trout, ready to feed on fly, usually lies fairly close to the surface. He will probably be keeping his position with quick, energetic flicks of the tail, rather than with slow, leisurely sweeps; he may, from time to time, veer a foot or two to one side so as to examine odd fragments brought down by the current, in the hope of finding food among them. There is a sort of electric look about him. He, too, will be more intent on his meal than on your approach, and you can usually reckon that he is a likely trout to catch.

Fish rising with cover close at hand—whether the cover consists of weeds, rocks or the river-bank—are often easier to approach than fish rising in open, unprotected stretches of water. They may feel that with cover nearby they have a quick escape-route from their enemies and can feed more confidently. At any rate, if I see a trout rising under the bank or right up against a weed-patch, I am inclined to bargain on getting a little closer up to him than I would otherwise. Perhaps for the same reason, trout in carriers or narrow streams will sometimes allow fishermen to come nearer to them than trout in broad rivers do.

There is an old fishing expression 'fine and far off', which may have cost fishermen a good many trout. Casting for a trout from farther away than is strictly necessary is a bad idea. The cast will be that much less delicate, and when you strike to drive the hook home, you will do it less well. It is always difficult to strike with a long length of line lying between the rod and the fish. The only man I knew who consistently hooked fish at very long range was Charles Ritz. Most of us can't. There is really very little point in setting yourself exercises in long-distance casting if you can possibly help it.

Having decided from which spot you wish to cast for your trout, the next move is to get there. This may mean crawling or crouching for the last few yards if the trout in the river are particularly shy. And it may also mean making use of whatever cover there is on the bank in the way of vegetation. It is worth remembering that if you cast for a trout from in front of a bush, you may be even more invisible to him—because you do not show up against his skyline—than if you cast from behind it. Cover on the bank is an asset to stalking, but it has its disadvantages, too. Before casting, it is always well worth while looking behind to make sure that the line of the cast is clear of trees and bushes. Too often the leader or fly gets fouled-up in twigs, branches, tall thistles and so on, when a quick glance around could easily have avoided it. There is no better case of 'more haste, less speed' than in preparing to cast for the first time over a fish.

This is very true in another way, too. It is usually wise to treat your first cast purely as an experiment, and to drop it just behind the trout, instead of directly in front of him. A cast that falls short cannot possibly frighten him, but a cast that goes too far and shows him the line is bound to do so. Also, this preliminary cast tells you whether the *next* cast—which you hope will touch down neatly a few inches upstream of the trout—is going to be in any grave danger of 'dragging'.

'Drag' is one of the dry-fly fisherman's bugbears. An artificial fly should float downstream in exactly the same way as a natural fly. But when any part of the line or leader between rod and fly is carried along by the current faster than the fly itself, it pulls on the fly and drags it sideways across the surface. You may, for instance, be fishing for a trout rising in a quiet glide by the far bank, but between you and the far bank may be faster eddies. When these act upon the belly of the line the effect is very soon seen on the fly. It begins to skitter and skate across the top of the water, leaving a wake behind it.

Now no natural up-winged fly behaves like this. If a trout sees such a performance he will not take the fly and may well stop feeding. Even if the drag is not pronounced enough to cause a visible wake behind the fly, it may still make it float a little unnaturally, with the same effect on the trout. This invisible drag is responsible for many refused flies.

A fisherman can take certain steps to avoid drag when he has to, and these will be dealt with in the next chapter. But let us suppose for the moment that everything has been done perfectly. The fly is the right one. The trout has not been frightened during the stalk. Your cast has been accurate and there has been no drag. The sequel, in this case, should be quite the most exciting moment in dry-fly fishing—when the trout actually takes the fly. One second, there is the fly floating along. The next second it vanishes in front of your very eyes, having been sucked neatly and quickly beneath the surface. This is when you have to remember to strike.

The idea in striking is to raise the rod and tighten the line, deliberately but quite firmly—never hard enough to break the cast—so that you drive the hook home in the trout's mouth. ('Tighten' would be a better word than 'strike'.) But how often everyone tries to do just this, merely to find the fly sailing back overhead without having touched the trout at all! 'They're coming a bit short today' is the usual excuse.

But are they? If our fly is nearly the right one, but not quite, the trout may indeed come constantly short and never take it wholeheartedly. Often, however, the strike has merely been mis-timed. In shooting it is said that more birds are missed behind than in front. On the chalk streams, it is an axiom that more fish are missed by striking too fast than too slow.

Many fishermen build up for themselves an elaborate rule for striking. When a fish takes, some say 'One thousand, two thousand *three*—' and then strike. Others curb their impatience by chanting 'God save the *Queen*'.

None of these rules is a complete answer in itself, because all fish rise a little differently. I myself never pause consciously before striking. It is instinct, as much as anything, that tells you just when to strike. This is where a fisherman's feel of the situation can perhaps be compared with the 'hands' of a horseman. Sometimes you will find yourself missing fish after fish, and losing confidence steadily, so that you strike more and more wildly. But again, there will be days when you can do nothing wrong. Every time a trout rises to your fly, you know surely that you will hook him, and surely enough every time you tighten on a fish the steel goes in fairly and squarely.

There is, however, one good guide for striking, other than instinct. Whenever a trout takes a fly he has to close his mouth at some stage. That is the time to strike. Think what a trout does as he rises. He lets the current carry him backwards and upwards till his nose meets the surface. Then he takes the fly. Then he forces himself down and upstream to his original place. While he is forcing himself down after rising, his mouth must be tight closed, otherwise it would offer too much resistance to the water. Strike then, and you are very likely to hook him. If you strike earlier, you *may* hook him, because the fly can still catch in his open mouth—but the chances are not nearly so good. If the strike comes later, he may well have opened his mouth again, either to breathe or to get rid of his last unwelcome mouthful.

Now a trout rising in fast water closes his mouth sooner, and gets back to his position more quickly, than a trout in slow water. If not, he would be carried some way downstream and have to make more effort to swim back. A large trout usually tackles a fly at a more leisurely speed than a smaller one. A trout coming up for a fly from deep down moves faster than a trout lying near the surface, since he has a greater distance to travel. This is why in hill-streams, where the current is swift, where the trout are small, and where they do not take up stations near the top of the water so frequently as in the slow chalk-streams, you always have to strike very quickly.

What happens next? Imagine that the strike has been successful. The rod is a-hoop, and a sizeable trout is making off towards the far bank as fast as he can go, diving deep and taking out line from the reel. A good sign. A well-hooked trout usually plays deep, while a lightly hooked fish tends to thrash around on the top of the water. Anyway, your heart is in your mouth. Even the most phlegmatic person can hardly remain calm and unruffled during the first nerve-racking run of a strong fit fish. A young girl, whom my family knew fairly well, acquired a stepmother several years ago—a cool, witty, self-collected and sophisticated woman of whom she was scared stiff. Nothing could ever shake the stepmother's self possession—or so it seemed until father, daughter and stepmother all went on a fishing holiday to Scotland. On the first day the step-mother announced confidently that she needed no help from gillies or anyone; that she would find, hook, play and land her own salmon. So she walked off downstream. After an hour or two the girl followed her.

She came upon her stepmother just as she had actually hooked a salmon, and to her surprise heard this unshakeable woman saying over and over again: 'Please-God-let-me-land-this-salmon-and-I-promise-I'll-be-a-good-girl-as-long-as-I-live. Please-God—.' The salmon was landed, and of course the stepmother and her step-daughter then became the closest of close friends.

A trout is quite exciting enough, though he is smaller. If he is large enough to take out line, you may feel as if you have no control over him at all and there seems no earthly reason why you should ever land him. Playing a fish is not the most important part of dry-fly fishing, but a good few fish can be lost by bad playing. A fish has to tire himself out before he can be brought to the net. He can only do this against the tension you exert through the rod. This is one good reason for never, never losing contact with him if you can avoid it. If he runs towards you, you must recover the line by reeling in and take up the strain just as quickly as you can. Then he will tire soon. It has been shown that even a cross-channel swimmer can only last a very short time against the strain of a rod.

Another good reason for keeping up this constant contact with a trout is that although you may not be able to stop his rushes you can nearly always guide them. Left to himself, the trout may vanish into a clump of weeds or twirl the cast round a snag. The best way of turning him before he gets to one of these unpleasant places is to apply side-strain, which means pulling from the side with the rod held horizontally, rather than from the top. A trout swims by flexing his body sideways. So you can throw him off balance and change his course by pulling from the side. If you try walking towards a given point with someone tugging at you from the right or left, you will find it far less easy to keep your direction than if the tug is from straight behind.

There is a great deal to be said for the old golden rule of playing: 'Always keep your rod up'. The higher the rod-top is, the more control you have over your fish, because you can vary the tilt quickly in any direction to apply side-strain. Also the trout is less likely to break the leader, since the first force of his rushes will be absorbed by the bending of the rod. A trout should not really break the leader, ever. Or not unless he gets into the weed or around a snag. It is amazing how strong even a fine leader is. If you take your fly between your fingers and try to break your tackle by pulling against the spring of the rod, you will find it nearly impossible. Only a sharp jerk if the leader is attached to something firm will break it. Sometimes a break occurs through striking too vehemently. But normally it should never happen unless the leader is rotten or there is a faulty knot.

As a result it is sensible to treat the trout fairly roughly. Namby-pamby playing, when a trout is handled as if it were on the end of a gossamer thread, merely prolongs the agony for both parties concerned. If a fish is well hooked he will usually stay on despite any amount of bullying. If not, he will probably come off anyway. An old keeper who once taught me a great deal was so attached to this policy of 'treat 'em rough' that whenever I hooked a fish he used to shout: 'Hold 'un, sir; hold 'un! *Don't* let 'un run.' Sometimes he even used to put his hand on my reel to stop a large fish from taking out line. It was surprising how seldom we lost a fish. Now I think he carried matters a little too far. It is highly dangerous to put your hand on the reel when a fish is actually running. If he wants line, he should usually be indulged. But nevertheless, it is feasible and wise and humane to tire a fish quickly, to play him and not play with him.

Unfortunately, a hooked trout manages to bury himself in a weed-bed only too frequently. Some people believe—though I myself think it probably an old wives' tale—that when he does this he often hangs on to the weed with his mouth. You can haul at him with the rod as long as you like but you will seldom shift him. Try handlining him from a point downstream. Let out several yards of line from the reel until there is a long length of slack between you and the trout. Then pick up the line *between* the rod-tip and the trout so that you have a direct pull on your fish. But do not pull. Pluck gently. At the first pluck, you will feel nothing but the dead weight of the weed. At the third or fourth pluck you will feel something alive at the end. This is the trout beginning to kick free. After a few more plucks the fish will abandon the weed and come into open water. Then drop the line quickly, reel in the slack and go on playing the trout. For some reason, trout always seem to react in the right way to this plucking, and it is seldom long before they loosen their hold on the weed and come clear.

When the trout is tired out he can be landed. It may be relevant to state here a purely personal prejudice about landing-nets. I do hate the V-shaped collapsible ones that are so convenient to pack into suitcases. I am sure you often pay dearly for the convenience later, perhaps just when you want to land the best trout of your day. The mesh of the net may become inextricably entangled in the collapsed part of the 'V' and all the shaking and swearing in the world will not uncollapse it. One more disadvantage is that owing to the shape of the net you have to steer your fish in a certain direction over it to make use of its full width. Nor can you feel around in weed with it.

For myself, I infinitely prefer a round rigid frame. If you fish from a high bank the handle should be quite long—or telescopic—but if you fish from a low bank or wade, it can be much shorter. A net like this seldom lets you down. You can bring your fish into it from any angle or direction. And if by any chance a trout fails to come out of the weeds when you pluck the line, a net with a solid frame allows you to go and probe around for him in the weed-bed.

When you land a trout, it is wise not to swoop or scoop at him with the landing-net. You may hit the leader and break it, or knock him off the hook, or frighten him into making a last plunge which may gain him his freedom. All landing should be carried out with deliberate care. First, unless you are wading, you have to choose a spot on the bank where you can stand firmly, and where your net can reach the water easily. The water around should be clear of weeds and snags if possible.

Then you have to guide the trout towards this spot. In order not to tie yourself into knots, hold the rod in your upstream hand and the net in your downstream hand. These will be the right hand or left hand according to which bank of the river you are on. Sink the net gently a few inches beneath the water. Keep low while you are doing it, for the less a trout sees of you the less likely he will be to get panicky and kick loose. Then draw the beaten trout quietly over the net, without moving the net itself until the moment when you can simply lift it up from the water with your trout inside it. That is, if you want to keep him.

This may not always be the case, however. You may instead decide to give him his liberty—perhaps because he is undersized, perhaps because you have caught enough trout already, or perhaps simply because he looks so beautiful and has fought so well that you feel his reward should be life, not death. In any case, if you wish to release him, you will try to take the hook out without removing him from the water. But if, on the other hand, the thought of the delicious meal he will make prevails, together with the age-old hunting instinct that most of us have, you will lift him out gently and of course despatch him cleanly and quickly. If your trout is appreciated at table, it is no unfitting end for him.

That particular trout was rising steadily and was easy to spot. You knew exactly where he was. You were in fact 'fishing the rise'—which means casting only for fish you see feeding. 'Fishing the water' means casting where you think fish *may* be feeding. You will normally 'fish the rise' on streams such as southern chalk streams, which are rich in natural fly-life, and where you hope to see plenty of fish rising. But on many other streams, where there are fewer flies and fewer signs of trout on the feed, you will 'fish the water'. The trout may well rise readily when and if they see a fly—but you have to guess where they are.

And this won't be blind guesswork. Using your experience of trout and their habits, you will find yourself thinking where *you* would lie if you happened to be a trout. Soon your own intuition will be telling you where to put each cast, and you will more and more often have the satisfaction of being right. And predicting the 'lie' of a trout successfully is one of the greatest rewards of dry-fly fishing. Out goes your fly towards that smooth glide under an overhanging branch. It alights softly, floats down daintily. You can see it standing up proudly on its hackles—until suddenly it disappears in the middle of a series of those breath-taking rings. 'I *thought* so', you can say rather smugly, as you tighten on a trout.

Then there is still-water fly fishing. New man-made reservoirs, lakes and ponds are providing more opportunities for trout fishing every year. Wet flies and 'lures' account for many trout. But so do dry flies and 'nymphs'. Again you can 'fish the rise' or 'fish the water'—remembering always that trout in still water keep on the move, since there is no current to bring food to them.

Wherever you fish the dry fly, you will be able to enjoy the thrill of actually seeing the trout take your fly. Other forms of fishing bring their own rewards. But this—this one moment of watching the fly fulfill its purpose of deception—is the dry-fly fisherman's unique privilege.

CHAPTER 2

Casting Principles

If you look at a rising trout hovering just below the surface, he may remind you a little of a lightweight boxer. He usually feints from one side to the other, stemming the current with deft movements of his fins, body and tail. Though he keeps a vigilant watch all around him for most of the time, his eyes are mainly directed forwards and upwards so that he can catch an early view of any surface-food that floats within his reach. Every now and again a fly dances towards him on the top of the water. Then he tilts his head and shoulders up. The current gently takes charge of him, lifts him in the water and carries him backwards until his nose meets the little insect. The fly vanishes. The trout forces his head down again, swims back to his old place and leaves behind him only a series of ever-widening rings.

This is the sort of trout you can catch with the dry fly, and now, when he is feeding on flies, is just the right moment. But first, of course, you have to be able to cast the fly. How long does it take to learn how to cast? Probably not more than about ten or twelve hours. If you have never cast a fly before in your life, and you lay aside two half-hours a day to practise it, you should easily be able to catch a trout in a chalk stream inside a fortnight. You may not be an expert by then. When you try to cast into a stiff breeze you may get into one of those tangles that lead fly-fishermen so frequently to fall into blasphemy. You may cast fairly short distances only. Your wrist may begin to ache after a little. But you will be able to catch trout, and these matters will all right themselves quickly. The action of casting is a completely new experience for the muscles concerned, and until they become used to it they tend to protest and make heavy weather of the whole affair. Soon the action will become almost automatic and even a long line will go out smoothly.

No one, I think, has ever learned to cast properly out of a book. Nothing in the world can replace personal guidance here. The rhythm of casting is very different from swinging a golf-club, wielding a cricket-bat, cracking a whip or anything else. It is not really difficult but it is entirely unique, and unless you discover the feel of it at the outset, from someone who knows how to cast, you are liable to make the mistake of relating it to something you have done before. Then you are quite likely to go wrong.

So it is nearly always best, right at the outset, to find a friend who is prepared to give up a little time to passing on his own knowledge, or a professional who can give good lessons. Here are one or two hints, however, which may help to explain how casting works.

There are several separate styles of casting, each with its enthusiasts. They do not, however, differ from each other tremendously. They are all designed to make the fly do the same thing, so to understand the principles is more important than worrying about style.

It will help if you try to think of the *fly* on the end of the line and not merely of the rod itself. In most ball-games the object is to make the bat, racquet or club meet the ball at the correct angle with the correct force. Footwork, body-work, arm-work and hand-work all culminate at the end of the weapon. Casting a fly is another sort of thing altogether. Here, the rod is only a means to an end. It is used as a form of remote control to manipulate a length of line, and the item of equipment that really matters is the fly moving through the air several yards away. Waving a rod by itself does no good—it is the effect of the rod on the line and fly that makes a good cast or a bad cast.

The actual force a fisherman puts into casting is a good deal less important than the timing. He does not really cast the fly at all. The rod does. The spring in the rod gives the line its impetus. The fisherman merely controls the rod and helps it to do its work. When you were at school, did you ever flick those little balls of blotting-paper across your classroom with a ruler? If you remember, it was the released tension in the ruler that sent them flying so far—much farther than you could ever have thrown them by yourself without a ruler. The ruler had to be bent back to build up tension before it would flick forward successfully.

A rod works in very much the same way. It is the released tension

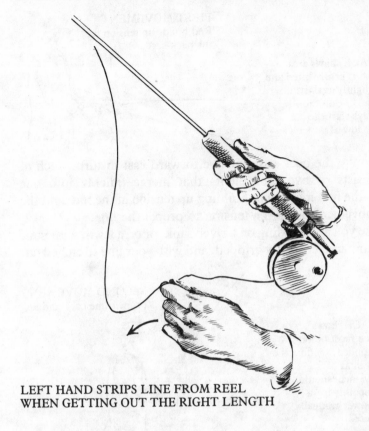

LEFT HAND STRIPS LINE FROM REEL
WHEN GETTING OUT THE RIGHT LENGTH

that propels the line. And the rod-tip—just like the top of the ruler—has to be flexed (or bent) to develop this tension. But whereas you used to bend the top of the ruler with your hand, the rod-tip is bent by the *weight of the line*.

Each complete cast consists of a backwards cast—or back-cast—and a forward cast. As the rod is lifted for the back-cast, it is bent by the weight of the line in front of you. This develops tension in the rod to propel the line backwards. Unless the rod does bend like this, it won't send the line back properly.

The same principle applies to the forward cast—but here the rod bends against the weight of the line *behind*. It is vital to remember that the rod has to do this. It explains one great truth about casting—that the back-cast is just as important as the forward cast. Unless the line goes well out behind, the rod won't flex when you bring it forward—and then the line won't go out in front.

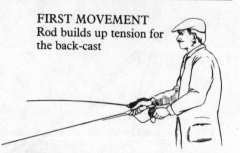

FIRST MOVEMENT
Rod builds up tension for
the back-cast

CLOCK-FACE shows area
in which rod is gently lifted and
will bend slightly against the
inertia of the line on the
water. Always start the
back-cast as low as possible.

Let us take the back-cast and the forward cast in turn. Each of these consists of two movements that merge quickly into one another—the first movement building up tension in the rod, and the second movement using the tension to propel the line.

Suppose you are standing on a river bank, or on a lawn, with your rod in your hand, correctly gripped, and with your line stretched out

SECOND MOVEMENT
propels line back and *up*

CLOCK-FACE shows
area in which most power
should be applied, sending the
line up as well as back.
Second movement should
continue smoothly from
first, with power gradually
being increased.

in front of you, either on the water or on the grass. The rod is pointing straight forwards, parallel to the ground. Your line must be stretched straight out—if it is to act immediately on the rod-tip. The first movement of the backward cast, then, is to raise the rod-tip slowly and gently. Before the rod overcomes the inertia of the line—before the line begins to move at all, in fact—the rod-tip will bend down a little.

This is the building up of the tension, the equivalent of bending back the ruler. As soon as you feel the line starting to gather speed, increase the strength of the action smoothly but very quickly. Using mainly your forearm—rather than your wrist—drive the line backwards and upwards. That, the second movement, is the same as actually flicking the ball of blotting-paper.

The whole force of the movement here should be directed into sending the line back and *up*. If the line travels straight back towards a spot no higher than the fisherman himself, he is likely to find his fly trying to hit him fair and square in the face. Even if the fly misses him the line will probably fall downwards to become entangled in the grass at his back before he can begin the forward cast. One good idea when you practise casting is to rig up a clothes-line behind you, five or six feet high.

Back and up. Always remember the 'up'. It is one of the things that newcomers to casting always find most difficult. Here are two hints about it. First, if the line is to travel back and up, so must the rod-tip. It is not a bad idea to watch the rod-tip occasionally while you are learning to cast. So long as it is travelling upwards, it will be sending the line upwards, but if you bring it too far back, it will let the line drop down. Try not to bring it back far beyond the vertical—that is, to a point above and only slightly behind your right shoulder.

Second, keep your wrist stiff until the very end of the back-cast. If you bend or 'break' your wrist too early, the rod-tip will begin going back instead of back and up. And the result, again, will be that the line starts falling behind you. Do all you can to keep your back-cast high.

Now for the forward cast. After you have driven the line backwards and upwards, pause. It is important to pause momentarily at this point. The purpose of the pause is to allow the line to stretch out behind you so that when you bring the rod forward again, the weight of the line behind will bend back the rod-tip. This is how tension is built up for the forward cast. While you pause you can let the rod-tip 'drift' a little further back—to give you more power when the time comes to push the line out in front.

How long should you pause? It will depend largely on the 'bendiness' of your rod and on the length of line beyond the rod-tip. The more flexible your rod, the longer it will take to develop and release tension. And the more line you have 'aerialised', the more time you have to allow for the pause.

The important thing is to pause until you know that the main weight of the line is behind you—you'll be able to feel the rod beginning to bend back—and also until you can sense that the line will soon lose its backwards impetus and start falling.

While the line still has a little backwards impetus left in it, begin

CLOCK-FACE shows how during pause the rod-tip can be allowed to 'drift' back a little – to 1 o'clock or even 2 o'clock – in preparation for the forward cast.

PAUSE
at the vertical, or very little beyond it, while main weight of line stretches out behind

the forward cast. You will soon be able to tell when the exact moment has come. This question of timing is three quarters of the secret in learning how to cast. When the moment arrives, start the forward movement fairly slowly again, building up tension against the weight of the line behind, but speeding it up very quickly indeed—using both wrist and forearm—so that the rod propels the line out forcefully in front of you. Aim for a point two or three feet above water-level. This action has sometimes been aptly described as 'knocking a nail into a tree on the opposite bank.' The line should not be cast *onto* the water—but into the air above the water. It must have time to straighten out, so that the fly can fall feather-light of its own accord on to the surface.

CLOCK-FACE
shows area in which tension is built up.

THIRD MOVEMENT
Build up tension for forward cast, starting gradually

FOURTH MOVEMENT
Push or 'top' line well out in front. Release
line in left hand, 'shooting' it through the rod-rings
for extra distance. The action is very similar to
tapping a nail into a tree with a hammer

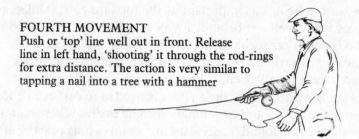

This is a description of one single cast from the time you start to lift the fly from the water to the time it settles there once more. When you actually fish for trout, you usually do a certain amount of 'false casting'. You cast the fly backwards and forwards in the air without allowing it to drop on the water. This is useful for several reasons. False casting dries the fly, allows you to get out line, and helps you to judge where the fly will finally fall. Too much false casting is foolish, however. Till your fly is on the water it cannot catch trout.

Do not let me leave the impression here that all the movements in casting are completely separated from one another. This is not so. There may be a distinct pause between the backward and forward cast, but the two movements in each—the building-up-tension movement and the sharper pushing or pulling movement—always blend smoothly into each other.

Finally, what does your left hand do? This hasn't been covered yet, and it is not essential to the main task of getting the rod to propel the line and fly. But your left hand still has an important part to play. While your right hand controls the *rod*, your left hand controls the *line*—holding it between the reel and bottom ring of the rod. You use it to strip line out from the reel in preparation for casting. Then, while you are false casting, you can use it to pull or 'haul' at the line so as to increase line-speed. And last of all, you can use it to release the line at the end of your final cast—so that a few more yards will 'shoot' through the rod-rings for extra distance.

These, however, are only elaborations on a basic principle. At the outset the action of casting may well seem strange. The rod may seem a decidedly unwieldly implement while the line appears to take on a life of its own. As for the fly, it will probably show an aptitude for getting hooked into practically anything except trout. Then, after a week or so, the entire operation begins to fit together. The backward cast is seen to be just as important as the forward cast. (Unless the line goes really well out behind, it will never go well out in front). The body, arm, wrist, hand, rod, line, leader and fly all suddenly become part of a whole. Each does its own fair share of the work and no more. (Casting, all at once, becomes effortless.)

It is really amazing how little effort is needed to cast even a long line, once the timing and co-ordination come easily. Whereas at one time you may have found it necessary to give up casting practice after only half an hour, because your arm and wrist began to cry out for a sling, you now suddenly discover you can cast for hours without feeling tired. Also you can master quickly most of the more advanced tricks of casting—tricks like stretching out line against wind, casting backhand, casting underhand, or shooting line—because they are all variations of the same basic theme. The delicate dropping of a fly within a distant square foot of water, a feat that seemed almost miraculous once, becomes a mere matter of course in a very short time.

Good casting is not only a matter of distance. Good 'presentation' is frequently, perhaps even usually, just as important or more so. Good presentation is the skill of making line, leader and fly fall gently on the water, all in a straight line, and exactly where you want them. If they do not fall straight, the trout may catch sight of the line. And when you strike, contact will be too slow. Indeed the value of casting a very long way is all too often over-rated. It can certainly be useful on large still waters where fish lie far out. But even on those waters it is probable that more trout are caught within a distance of fifteen yards than outside it. A badly-presented fly—particularly a dry fly—will very, very seldom be taken by a trout. And the farther you try to cast, the more difficult you will find it to present a fly really well.

To present a fly well against a wind is never easy. Brute force doesn't help a great deal. If you try to overcome a wind merely by casting harder, you may succeed in driving out the line but you will not get over the real difficulty, which is that the lighter leader and fly will be blown back towards you. The way to avoid this is certainly not to strain at your casting.

When faced by a wind, try cutting your line down on to the water instead of aiming into the air above it. Then the wind has less time in which to affect the fly. And if you pull a little line *back* through the rings with your left hand, this helps to straighten out the leader.

With some trial and error you will soon be able to cast into a fair breeze. A howling headwind, unfortunately, can sometimes make good casting virtually impossible unless you discover a sheltered spot or some stretch of the river where the wind is behind you.

Then there are certain ways in which casting can minimise the chance of drag. Drag, if you remember, is set up when the line is swept downstream faster than the fly and begins pulling the fly sideways across the surface. A very accurate cast, which puts the fly only a few inches upstream of the trout, sometimes prevents drag, when it might otherwise have happened. By the time the fly reaches the trout the belly of the line has not yet had an opportunity to become a nuisance.

But sometimes other measures are needed. Where the set of the current is really inconvenient, drag may start almost immediately. In these circumstances you should throw a deliberately crooked line. People who are finding out how to cast often become a little confused here, and no-one can blame them. First of all they learn how to throw a nice straight line; then, apparently, they are told to forget all about it and start doing the opposite. Nevertheless, where there is any fear of drag, an absolutely straight line can be a liability. The current may begin to set up drag as soon as the line and fly hit the water. The best sort of cast, when you meet this situation, is one that makes the line land in a curve or zigzag on the surface.

If, for instance, you jerk or wriggle the rod-top right at the end of your cast just before the fly drops, the line, too, will fall in a series of wiggles. The current has to straighten them out before it can drag the fly. So you gain a certain amount of time during which you hope that the fly will pass over the fish and be firmly taken. Putting an upstream curve into the line, as it lands on the water, is another useful accomplishment, and not too hard to learn. But these accomplishments—which in any case apply only to rivers and not to still water—all come into the category of 'advanced casting' and you can catch plenty of trout without them.

Good casting is a pleasure in itself. It is what attracts many people to flyfishing. I know of at least one fisherman who casts beautifully but who has a habit of seldom leaving his fly long enough on the water for trout to take it. He is fully aware of this. 'I know I'd catch many more trout if I left it floating longer', he says, 'but then I wouldn't be able to cast so often, would I'?

Preliminary note on tackle:

At this stage most books on any kind of fishing tend to give an account of the sort of tackle you are likely to need for it. But I have an idea that just now a break with convention might be fairly sensible—so I have left all the information you may care to have about tackle till Chapter 13. If you thirst for the information right away, please go straight there. But my reason for leaving any examination of suitable tackle till later on is that it simply cannot help being rather technical. You may not, however, feel like becoming involved in technicalities at the moment. You may well prefer to read about trout and about the food of trout and about catching trout, which is how we now continue. But you can always turn to Chapter 13 immediately if you wish. The choice, as it should be, is yours.

Trout, Trout Waters and Flies

PART TWO

Trout Waters and Flies

CHAPTER 3

His Lordship

There is only one species of trout native to the British Isles, and his Latin name is *Salmo trutta*, a name which used to be reserved for sea trout alone. While you often hear about brown trout, gillaroo trout, slob trout, lake trout and so on, as well as sea trout, it is now definitely believed that all these are just different varieties of the same fish—*Salmo trutta*. The changes in colour, markings and size have been brought about by their varying environments.

The native trout we usually fish for inland is called a brown trout, and he spends his whole time in fresh water. The sea trout, on the other hand, is born in fresh water but travels down to the sea as soon as he is old enough to make the journey. Then he lives and grows in salt water and only comes back into fresh water to spawn. How two members of exactly the same species developed such contrary habits may always be a mystery. One possible theory is that the brown trout once lived in the sea. When the ice-packs retreated from Southern Europe, many of the trout found the seas too warm for them and sought refuge in the cooler waters of freshwater rivers, where some were afterwards landlocked in lakes. But it is just as likely that our present sea trout once lived in fresh water and migrated at some stage to richer feeding-grounds in the oceans.

Another sort of trout which you may catch is the rainbow trout (*Salmo gairdneri*). The rainbow is a different species altogether, and he is not a native of the British Isles but was originally imported in 1884 from the western seaboard of North America. He does not breed very well in this country, and there are only a few rivers here in which he has reproduced naturally and established himself. (The Derbyshire Wye and Buckinghamshire Chess are two of them.)

But to make up for this, he has turned out to be very useful for 'stocking' purposes once he has been artificially reared. Although he only lives about half as long as a brown trout, he grows about twice as quickly. This means that he is rather cheaper to rear to a catchable size. Many reservoirs and other waters are now stocked with a high proportion of artificially-bred rainbows—and when you hook one you soon discover why they have earned such a high reputation as 'acrobats' on the end of a line.

This borrowing of the rainbow from America has by no means been a one-way affair. The Americans in their turn began importing the brown trout from Europe at the end of the last century, and they found that he had no trouble in reproducing naturally there.

Brown trout have also been taken to many other countries—as far apart as India and New Zealand—and have nearly always proved themselves first-rate, hardy colonists.

Trout, biologically speaking, are 'vertebrate animals', or 'back-boned animals'—just as human beings are—but with fins instead of limbs and able to breathe in water. They do this by taking in water through their mouths, then passing it out through their gills. Tiny blood-vessels in the gill filaments—those red flaps you will find inside their gill covers—extract some of the oxygen dissolved in the water and pass it into their bloodstream. This is why the trout you see in rivers always lie in the same direction, facing the current. If they faced downstream in flowing water it would flow the wrong way through their breathing system and they would literally drown.

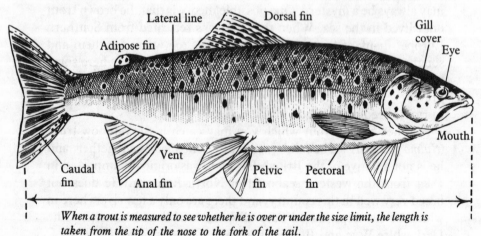

Lateral line · Dorsal fin · Gill cover · Eye · Adipose fin · Mouth · Caudal fin · Vent · Anal fin · Pelvic fin · Pectoral fin

When a trout is measured to see whether he is over or under the size limit, the length is taken from the tip of the nose to the fork of the tail.

And this is also why, when dry-fish fishermen walk along a river bank looking for rising trout, they nearly always walk upstream. Then they can be reasonably certain of approaching a fish from behind with a much better chance of seeing him before he sees them.

Even at the best of times, however, trout are not particularly easy to see because they have a valuable gift for blending their colouring to match their backgrounds. They can change their colour and markings by the concentration or dispersal of light and dark pigments in their skin. Of course, they do not make quite such a good job of it as the chameleon, and they take a good deal longer about it—but still, this colour-blending is very useful. The pigments rearrange themselves according to the light rays reaching the trout's eyes from underwater objects. So blind trout often become black or dark in colour.

A trout's senses are tremendously important to fishermen, and the rest of this chapter will be spent in explaining them. The eyesight of a trout probably influences dry-fly fishing more than any of his other senses. A trout's eyes are on either side of his head. They do not always have to look to the front, as our eyes do, so he has a much

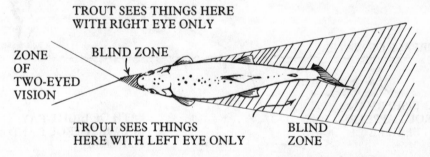

TROUT SEES THINGS HERE
WITH RIGHT EYE ONLY

ZONE
OF
TWO-EYED
VISION

BLIND ZONE

TROUT SEES THINGS
HERE WITH LEFT EYE ONLY

BLIND
ZONE

greater range of vision; but his eyesight within this range is perhaps not so precise, since he can see most things with only one of his eyes and has very little two-eyed, or binocular vision—so vital to the judging of distance.

The scope of a trout's vision can be seen in the drawing above. Just behind his back he has a blind area—the advantages of approaching him from down-stream become even more obvious. To his left and his right there are large one-eyed or monocular areas, while in front he has a fairly limited two-eyed area where he can judge distance very well.

When you stalk a trout from the side he can only see you with one eye, so he finds it very difficult to tell exactly how far away you are. If you approach him in a straight line he will seldom be frightened because there seems to him to be little apparent change in the landscape. If you make a sideways movement, however, he can see it much more quickly and may be off in a flash.

Interestingly enough, fish like the trout, which not only catch but often have to pursue their prey, usually have their eyes set farther forward in their heads than other fish. In this way they sacrifice a certain amount of the view behind them so that they can gain a wider range of two-eyed vision in which to judge distance and hunt effectively.

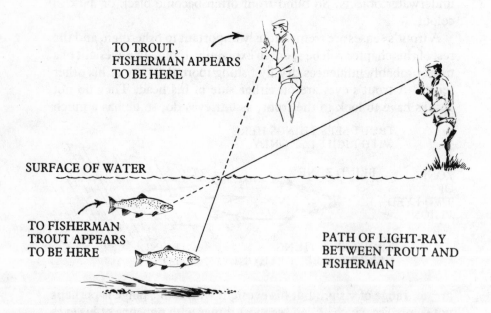

TO TROUT, FISHERMAN APPEARS TO BE HERE

SURFACE OF WATER

TO FISHERMAN TROUT APPEARS TO BE HERE

PATH OF LIGHT-RAY BETWEEN TROUT AND FISHERMAN

A trout's sight of things above the water is largely governed by the refraction of lights as it meets the surface. The eyesight of trout, like our own, depends upon the fact that the eye can pick up rays of light travelling towards it from anything within view. Now, all light rays entering the water from the air, or vice versa, are refracted. They are bent downwards. If you place a half-crown in a basin, put the basin on a table and then stand back a little from the table, the rim of the basin will eventually hide the half-crown. But if someone fills up the basin with water while you are standing there, a small miracle seems to occur. The half-crown again becomes visible. You are actually looking at a point just above the half-crown, but the refracted light rays allow you to see over the rim.

You can imagine this effect from the point of view of a trout just beneath the surface. The diagram shows it. Now imagine *all* the light rays coming to him in this way—remembering also that light striking the water from an angle of less than ten degrees is nearly all reflected *from* the surface. The result is as shown in the diagram below.

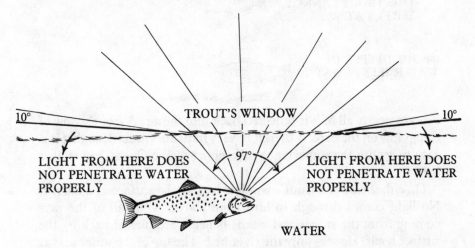

TROUT'S WINDOW

10°   10°

LIGHT FROM HERE DOES
NOT PENETRATE WATER
PROPERLY

97°

LIGHT FROM HERE DOES
NOT PENETRATE WATER
PROPERLY

WATER

Everything a trout sees above the water is crowded into a small window in the surface, which is usually called the 'trouts' window'. He can *only* see through his window. The light rays which hit the water outside his window do not come to his eye at all. The deeper the trout is in the water, the larger his window becomes and the more he can see.

So if you come upon a trout lying only just below the surface of the water you can take it for granted that he will notice a good deal less of what is happening above it than a trout rather further down. However, if a trout goes too deep down, particularly in cloudy water, he will not see you at all clearly because the water itself absorbs light. Light rays cannot penetrate very far into it without losing their strength.

Again whenever light strikes the surface of the water some of it is always reflected back into the air. It never gets as far as the trout's eye—and the lower the starting point of the light, the less of it actually goes into the water. This is why fishermen always keep low on the river bank. If a ray of light comes to the water from directly above, most of it passes into the water. Of a ray meeting the surface at an angle of 45 degrees, about half passes in. But at an angle of 10

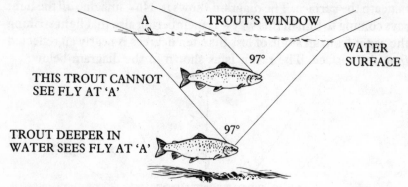

degrees nearly all of it is reflected back into the air. A trout's view of things low on the bank is therefore very indistinct indeed, so that it is easy to realise the importance of keeping well down as you stalk a fish.

On either side of a trout's window he sees the surface as a mirror. No light comes through to him from above, while all of the rays coming from the stones and weeds beneath are turned back by the surface itself. He sees only the river bed. The top of the water acts as a complete ceiling of mirrors, except for that one circular window directly above, through which the trout gets a rather blurry view of air and land, distorted by distance and the refraction of light, and perhaps by ripples or eddies on the surface.

When you cast a floating fly to a trout it is well worth remembering that he cannot notice anything outside his window on the surface. So if you take care to let neither your line nor the thicker part of your leader float into the window you are less likely to frighten him than if you do. Unless your fly itself does float into it, however, he will ignore your offering completely, simply because he cannot see it. Things below the water he can see clearly. He can see a sunk fly at a far greater distance than a floating fly because it is on the near side of his ceiling of mirrors. He will often, for instance, come quite a long way to take a sunk wet fly or nymph, far further than he would for a true dry fly.

When you come to choose flies yourself it is useful to know something about the trout's ability to distinguish between different colours and sizes. Fortunately, some recent research has filled in certain gaps in our knowledge. Some people say that trout are colour-blind. Therefore, they maintain, the colour of a fly doesn't matter. Scientists, however, have proved them wrong. Trout may not see the same spectrum as we do. They may see more colours, or fewer colours, but it's been shown that like most fish they can distinguish colour differences.

Some fish, for instance, if they are fed exclusively on a diet of blood-worms, can easily be taken in by bits of red wool, but not by blue wool, green wool or yellow wool. Again, if you feed them the whole time through blue eye-droppers, they will soon learn to swim to blue eye-droppers even if they are empty. They will not swim towards empty eye-droppers of any other colour. Many tests like this have indicated that fish do have a sense of colour—while other tests, using shades of grey, have shown that this seems to be quite separate from their sense of shade and brightness.

How about size? Most fishermen have known plenty of days when a change in the size of their fly has been more effective than a change in the pattern. Size can certainly be very important. And shape? Tame carp, again, have shown in tests that they can distinguish between triangles, circles and squares. But then carp, by nature, approach their food slowly and have a certain amount of time to look at it. Trout take their food at a fair speed, and in their case it is quite possible that the general appearance of a fly, as the light shines through it, or perhaps the motion given to it by the current or its own strugglings, is at least as important as its exact shape.

Certainly an old, well-chewed, battle-worn fly often seems just as tasty to trout as a brand-new one with not a feather out of place. It seems fair to say that although the general outline, colour and translucency of a fly—and the way it rides on the water—are noticed by the trout, they very seldom bother to examine the more tiny details of it.

Luckily, trout do not always seem to make full use of their powers of perception and judgement. Sometimes they seem so bemused by hunger or, for all we know, by spring fever or mid-summer madness, that they snap up nearly any apology for a fly. On these so-called duffers' days the school of any-fly's-as-good-as-the-next comes home happy. On days of a different sort, all the trout in the river seem gifted with an uncanny genius for telling artificial flies from the natural ones. Then the fly-maker's art really comes into its own. Good flies—flies tied skilfully from carefully selected materials—will always look more like the real thing than bad ones do, because they let through the right kind of light, because they dance on the water and because they somehow appear to be alive.

During the evening, as the light fades, you may find that you can get rather closer to your trout than you could in broad daylight. But since the trout has a special apparatus in his eye which enables him to see in dim light better than human beings can, it is as well not to overdo this. Only too often trout see us perfectly well when we never catch a glimpse of them. It might be a little disturbing to know how many feeding trout we frighten each time we walk up a river bank. Sometimes they leave bow-waves behind them as they dash away. More often, perhaps, they just sink very quietly down in the water, and leave us no indication of the opportunities we may have missed.

Trout may see less well when they look into the sun than when they look away from it. They cannot contract the pupil of their eye quickly, and may tend to be dazzled, whereas if they look in the other direction they can see objects on the surface clearly against the sky. So if you fish for trout with the sun behind you, you may have a slight advantage. But then take care to remember that a trout is always very frightened when the shadow of a fisherman falls across his window.

So much for the trout's vision. Now for his hearing. There is an old myth that fishing wives are never allowed to speak to their husbands because it might frighten the fish. So far as trout-fishing is concerned this is quite untrue. Most trout will seldom be scared even by a pistol-shot on the bank.

Trout can hear, however. All hearing consists of sensing vibrations, and a trout can certainly sense vibrations in the water, even if these start in the air. He has hidden ears of a sort, and he can also hear with his lateral line, the long line running down each side of his body. This is sensitive to vibrations, too. Stamping around on a river bank or banging about in a boat, therefore, is never a good idea, and if wading is necessary nothing can be lost by moving in the water as delicately as possible.

On the other hand, aeroplanes have been breaking the sound-barrier nearly every day recently just by the little stream I fish in

Hampshire. Although the bangs have created a great uproar among the local cattle and pheasants, I cannot say that I have ever known a trout affected by them. If the trout happened to be feeding at the time, they continued to feed. That is only my own experience, however. It has been proved that some laboratory fish are very good at distinguishing different sounds, and therefore it is probably wise to play safe and avoid too much racket on the bank. Even so, it is extremely unlikely that trout will ever be frightened by a wife's conversation—or even by the habitual cursing of dry-fly fishermen when things go wrong.

Like some human beings, fish can develop certain senses at the expense of others. The trout hunts by eyesight so, quite naturally, his vision is better than his senses of taste and smell. Yet a trout has smell-buds in his nostrils. Biologically there is no reason why a trout should not have a sensitive sense of smell if he finds it useful. Nocturnal feeders such as dog-fish track down their food almost entirely by smell, and it is quite possible that large old trout, who often hunt by night, have also learned to smell fairly well. The majority of trout, however, probably do not smell their food before they eat it, particularly in fast water.

Trout have taste-buds, too, concentrated chiefly in their mouths but also scattered all over their skin. Though human beings can only taste in their mouths, many fish—the goldfish is one—can taste over their entire outer surfaces. It has been shown that fish are capable of distinguishing between sweet, salt, sour and bitter. (Without a sense of smell to help us, these are the only tastes we can distinguish ourselves.) Often and often a trout will pick out a particular sort of fly on the water when there are many larger flies hatching at the same time. There seems absolutely no reason why this should not be due to the fact that smell and taste combine to make some flies more palatable.

All fish have an acute sense of temperature; they can detect even small variations very quickly. Every fish has a normal range of temperature that lets him live comfortably. In the case of some fish this range includes high temperatures, and in the case of others fairly low ones, but in either case a fish can only stay alive within its own particular limits. It quickly dies if these are overstepped. Trout begin to be in danger when the water-temperature is in the seventies.

When trout farmers transfer young trout from cans to a river, they

—33—

always spend some time bailing water slowly out of the cans and replacing it with river water so that any small change in temperature takes place gradually and does not distress the fish. Sudden changes of temperature, even within their temperature range, often harms them. In warm weather trout go to the cooler parts of a lake or river, only returning to the shallower parts with colder weather.

That is a brief résumé of the trout's physical senses. Perhaps it is worth mentioning that the experts consider it more or less impossible for fish to experience pain on anything like the same scale as we do. Here is a comforting thought for fishermen.

There is one further aspect. You will often hear trout described as artful, cunning and resourceful. This is far too flattering. No trout thinks. His behaviour is usually dictated purely by instinctive responses, although these may have been influenced a little by his own experiences. If he takes the dry fly you offer him he does so because this is his response to something that looks like food at a time when he is hungry. If he refuses it he does so because it does not look like the food he wants. Probably he is not even frightened. He may have learned from experience that unnatural-looking insects with fibres trailing from their noses are not particularly edible, but he certainly does not work out that anyone is trying to catch him. Similarly, when a trout breaks your cast in the weeds or round some sunken roots he does so only because he has found that his best response to any strange danger is to seek the nearest refuge. A trout's brain is very small. It is sometimes said that dry-fly fishermen 'pit their brains against those of the trout'. No-one has ever levelled a bigger insult at us.

CHAPTER 4

His Element

Trout always like living—and grow best—where there is plenty of food. Water in itself is a rather inhospitable element, because pure water, distilled water, contains no nourishment for any living plants or animals, let alone trout. Fortunately the water in lakes and rivers is not pure—it has collected from the ground certain substances called salts. The salts—which go by names like phosphate, sulphate and nitrate—are usually dissolved in the water, though sometimes they exist in particles of earth carried along by the current. If there are plenty of them the water is called rich, and if there are rather few it is usually described as poor. Salts are the earliest link in the food-chain and support the first living things, which are plants. Big plants and small plants alike live on the salts. The smallest plants are the algae—microscopic green or blue-green vegetables that either float around in still water, without roots at all, or moor themselves firmly to under-water objects. Incidentally, the film that covers most sunken stones and weeds consists of millions of these minute algae.

The algae are the food of many tiny animals, including insects—such as the larvae of the flies which trout feed on—and these in turn are eaten by larger and larger animals, till the trout is reached. This food-chain is even carried on outside the water, when water-creatures nourish land animals or birds. In the end the dead animals and plants sink to the bottom where, if they are not eaten by other animals which feed by scavenging, their bodies are attacked by bacteria. Bacteria break down their corpses into the original materials from which they were built up so that the materials are let loose again in the water and help to make it even richer.

Wherever the water is rich, thousands of creatures of different sorts and sizes will live in it. It becomes like a jungle in miniature.

The richer the water, the more creatures there will be. All of them play a part in the food-chain. Nearly all of them, if they are not trout food themselves, are the food of the trout's food, or perhaps even the food of the trout food's food, and in the end they all rely on the dissolved salts in the water.

So rich water usually breeds the fattest trout, though poor water—provided other conditions are right—may provide a home for quite a number of small ones. In general, hard or alkaline waters are rich in nutrient salts and soft or acid waters rather short of them. Mountain streams that flow over hard rock or through barren soil have little chance to pick up valuable salts and are therefore usually acid. Hard, unfertile country produces soft waters which are usually also acid—like the small streams of Scotland and Cornwall. These waters may have plenty of trout in them, but the scarcity of food will prevent them growing very big. An alkaline stream of the same size, say in Hampshire, will be richer in food and more prolific as regards large trout. Both chalk and limestone districts can usually be counted upon for particularly good fishing waters—partly because rivers and lakes there have a very good supply of a substance called calcium, which always helps to enrich the water.

Oxygen is as essential to trout as food is. All underwater animals breathe oxygen, as land animals do, and a fish out of water dies not because there is less oxygen in the air—actually there is more—but because his special way of breathing is only suited to extracting oxygen from water. All water contains some oxygen; but since the animals are constantly using it up the supply needs continual replenishing. This can happen in various ways.

A little oxygen seeps very slowly through the surface from the air, and where the current is fast and the surface choppy the water mixing with the air hastens the process. Well-aerated water, like the water in a pool beneath a waterful, is usually full of oxygen—and often full of trout. But the most useful means of all is through the action, once more, of plants.

All plants, during the day, go through the process of photo-synthesis. That is, they breathe in carbon dioxide from the water and use it for their own nourishment. Then they breathe out oxygen. Scientists know very little about how this process actually works except that a green pigment called chlorophyll plays a large part in it, but on a fine, sunny day you can often see the bubbles of oxygen coming up from underwater plants.

Thanks to photosynthesis, plants can contribute a great deal of the oxygen used by trout and other water animals; these, in return, breathe out the carbon dioxide used by plants. During the night, however, plants take in oxygen and give out carbon dioxide like animals, because photosynthesis can only take place under light. Even so, green plants nearly always produce, on balance, more than they absorb.

The store of oxygen in any stretch of trout water can be seriously endangered by several causes. The warmer water gets, the less oxygen it can hold. And decomposing matter, like dead leaves, animal corpses, or sewage, takes up oxygen very quickly. De-oxygenation is often caused by pollution, always a very real theat to country-lovers, whoever they may be.

Pollution takes two common forms, the worst of which is the dumping in the river of sewage or other decomposing waste matter. Decomposition on such a large scale can easily rob the water completely of oxygen. The other, less usual type of pollution, is neither more nor less than direct poisoning, when a factory or farm discharges lethal chemicals. Both sorts of pollution can be fatal, but happily the laws of the country, plus the work of the Angler's Co-operative Association and other bodies, do give a measure of protection against pollution. Even so, we can never have too much protection—if we want our grandchildren to be able to fish, or even to paddle safely.

There are, however, other dangers. As an example, imagine a small pond, full of vegetation, on a still, warmish autumn day. Dead leaves have fallen into it and are absorbing oxygen. Perhaps, to make matters worse, some unlucky animal has drowned in the pond and is using up even more oxygen while bacteria decompose its carcase. Despite all this, the waterplants have produced enough oxygen during daylight to sustain life in the pond.

When night comes—particularly if it is a warm night—the situation may change for the worse. Suddenly the plants, instead of producing oxygen, are competing for it themselves. In a few hours the pond may become uninhabitable, but there is no escape for the animals in it and by the time morning arrives many of them may be dead. Here is one of Nature's often-unnoticed tragedies. If you own a goldfish pond in your garden you should take care to clean the dead leaves out of it when autumn comes. The goldfish, however, has one peculiar characteristic—he needs less oxygen than any other fish. That is why you can keep him in a bowl with no plants growing. Trout, on the other hand, like more oxygen than many fish and always thrive in the best oxygenated places.

The oxygen content of larger ponds, and of lakes, seldom goes through such wild fluctuations. On a wide open sheet of water the wind helps to mix the water with the air. In a river the current achieves the same end, and the flowing water helps to keep the temperature fairly constant.

Food and oxygen are the two most important things in life to a trout. And because of this, food chains and oxygen chains are vitally important to trout water. It is well worth understanding how they both operate. A very simple example, on a small scale, can be seen in any ordinary water-butt filled with rainwater.

Rainwater is fairly pure, and therefore poor in salts, but it collects just enough of them on its journey through the air to support small colonies of algae. After the water has been standing for a little, a greenish film will start appearing on the sides of the butt. This is made by algae, beginning to establish themselves in a new-found home. Shortly afterwards some tiny animals will arrive to feed on the tiny plants. You will have to look very carefully to see them with the naked eye, but a fine muslin net drawn through the water will collect thousands of them. These are the pioneers of the animals. Sometimes they do quite well, build a highly successful empire and may attract some larger animals. But all too often they are much too greedy for their own good. They attack the algae and reduce them to the point where they can no longer release enough oxygen for the little world of the water-butt. The world dies. The whole cycle has to start all over again.

On a larger scale, exactly the same principles are at work in any trout-stream or any lake. It is easy to see how useful water plants are. The smallest of them—the algae—provide food for the smallest animals, and without small animals there will be no big ones. The bigger plants are themselves covered with algae, and all the plants help to oxygenate the water. Also, of course, they give shelter to trout and trout-food.

Most of the water plants that grow to any size are called weeds, but whereas 'weeds' are ruthlessly eliminated in a garden, a good growth of weeds in a river is something to encourage. They only become a nuisance when they're the wrong kind or when extra-rich water makes them grow too thickly. Where they are too profuse they may cause a danger of flooding or stagnation, or collect too much mud round their roots, or leave too little open space for fishing. At this stage they have to be cut back.

Any water can be 'farmed'. Just as a farmer prefers fertile soil, a fisherman prefers fertile water, rich in nourishment for trout. As a farmer grows useful plants and gets rid of others, a fisherman can encourage the weeds that provide the best food and shelter for trout and do away with the rest. If the current is too fast for plants to root themselves properly, he can always slow it up by erecting little dams and groynes. If, on the other hand, the current is so slow that mud is deposited on the bottom, killing the weeds, he can make it faster, and also clean the river-bed, by concentrating the flow between hurdles, or in some other way. Then he can improve his stock of trout by increasing their supply of natural food, even to the extent of protecting or rearing the animals that they eat. Wherever there is plenty of food and oxygen, and a fairly even, cool water temperature too, trout will live and breed and thrive.

CHAPTER 5

His Life

Food and enemies

Some weeks before Spring, young trout hatch from their eggs. They are funny-looking creatures, these freshly-hatched 'alevins'—about half-an-inch long, with round, monstrous eyes and huge bag-like affairs slung underneath their bellies. The bags are actually yolk-sacs, full of nourishment, which the trout gradually absorb during their first three or four weeks after hatching. At this time they seldom feed through their mouths at all, they have no scales, they are smaller than sticklebacks, and they may easily fall a prey to eels, fish, dragonfly nymphs or any creature larger than themselves. There are a great many of these creatures, so it is hardly surprising that only one alevin out of hundreds ever becomes an adult trout.

The little alevins hide themselves in the stones or gravel among which they hatched from the egg. For about three weeks they live in the 'redds'—as the places where trout lay their eggs are called—and subsist on their yolk-sacs. Towards the end of this time they begin making sorties into the stream, learning how to face the current and recognise food when they see it.

As his yolk-sac disappears an alevin starts to resemble a miniature trout. He is now a 'fry', with well-developed fins and pigmented skin. Soon the 'platelets' of the scales will appear. The fry takes up a position in the current and feeds on the small morsels which it brings him—morsels such as fly-larvae and young shrimps.

At this stage the difference between large and small trout first begins to show. A trout's rate of growth as compared with his fellows depends entirely upon the force and energy with which he hunts. Competition among trout-fry is ruthless, and the strongest and hungriest fry will always get the best food, shouldering the others out of the way. These bullies will grow best. Quite a few of the weaker fry will starve, while many others will only grow very slowly.

All trout, including trout-fry, are carnivorous and support themselves by eating any other members of the animal kingdom they can find. Often young trout eat much the same type of food as their elders do. But whereas mature trout prefer mature flies, larvae, shrimps and snails, the young fish batten upon the baby ones. In lakes, or in the very quiet parts of a river, trout-fry feed also upon zoo-plankton. These are microscopic animals which either float or swim around in the water. Water-fleas are among the most important of them and they make excellent food for young fry. There are less zoo-plankton in rivers than in lakes because a current soon washes them away.

As soon as the alevins turn into fry, they start fighting for good lies in the water. As they grow older they take over better and better lies. Trout have no love for each other, and except during the spawning season, when they pair, they lead a selfish, solitary existence. They do not welcome companions gladly. A trout's home may consist of no more than a slight hollow in the river-bed, but even so he will quickly chase other fish out of it if possible. When trout go house-hunting they look for three things—good cover, easy lying and plenty of food. The first of these can be provided by rocks or by tree-roots, or by holes in the bank or by weeds. Easy lying often goes with good cover. A trout never likes to swim hard all day merely to keep himself in a static position against a strong current. Therefore he chooses places out of the direct flow, in weed-beds, behind stones or perhaps where the bottom dips a little so that the main force of the current passes overhead. In lakes the consideration of easy lying does not count nearly so much. But in both lakes and rivers there still remains the question of food supply. A trout in a river would far rather have his food brought to him by the stream than go searching for it. After all, the current does provide an excellent meal service twenty-four hours a day. So your trout, although he prefers living out of the current, will often choose a home fairly near it so that he can make a swift sortie from behind his stone to seize any animal that is being swept down, or else take up a station beside his weed-bed to be within easy reach of floating flies when they are hatching on the surface.

In still water the trout also live close to their food. This means that they will usually avoid the very deepest water, for the sun's light cannot reach down there and trout food will be pretty sparse. On the other hand very shallow water is too exposed for them. They will live mostly between the shallows and the deeps, hovering near the weed-beds, roaming the open water in search of zoo-plankton, or hunting the animals that live in clean gravel or shingle. If the level of the water in a lake changes, or if its flow in a river alters, the trout will frequently look for new homes to suit the new conditions.

At the end of a year a trout becomes a yearling—no longer a fry. He is now an active little fish of four or five inches in length. He is sometimes called a fingerling. After two years, in a good chalk-stream, he is eight or nine inches long and it no longer takes a second look to pick him out from among the minnows. In the Spring of the next year he should be catchable—that is, twelve or thirteen inches long in a chalk stream, and nearly a pound in weight. A rainbow trout takes only two years to reach the same weight as a brown trout does in three, which makes him a far cheaper proposition for trout-farmers to rear.

The growth of trout is a good deal slower in streams less rich in food than the Test and Itchen and other chalk streams. In many West Country, Welsh, Irish and Scottish streams, a trout becomes catch-able when he is only a quarter of a pound and six or seven inches long. It will still, however, have taken him about three years to grow up if he is a brown trout. Generally speaking, in any stretch of water there is enough food to maintain x pounds' weight of trout. The nature of the food will often decide whether you have, say, ten two-pound trout or twenty one-pound trout or forty half-pound trout. Flies, if there are plenty of them, are quite good trout-food, but very few trout exist on flies alone. If, for instance, they can get freshwater shrimps and snails as well, they seem to find these particularly nourishing and will grow large quickly. Other food like small insect-larvae and zoo-plankton will support a number of small fish but will hardly ever raise them to any great size.

There may, of course, be other types of fish in the water competing with the trout for the available food. Coarse fish of nearly any sort will eat bottom-food that might have served to nourish trout. In clear, fast, well-oxygenated water the trout have an advantage over the coarse fish and breed faster than the coarse fish, but in other types of water the coarse fish, once introduced, establish themselves fairly quickly and may even start evicting the trout. Grayling and salmon-fry, as well as coarse fish, deplete the supplies of trout-food. Both of them rely on much the same diet as trout, and the more there are of them in the river, the more competition there will be for the food—a struggle in which many trout may come off badly.

Added to competitors are predators. A trout spends his whole life in perpetual danger of losing it through attack from either water or the air. He has several enemies in his own element, the most unpleasant of which is the pike. A pike can eat his own weight of trout very quickly if he is hungry.

Small trout are also very acceptable morsels so far as large trout are concerned. Trout of any size will catch and eat smaller fish whenever they can. Medium-size trout will pursue minnows, bullheads and trout-fry. So will larger trout—but they often snatch up yearling trout as well. As a trout grows bigger and stronger he is likely to prey more and more on other fish, since smaller mouthfuls of food are no longer enough to keep up his weight.

Then there are otters. A great deal of discussion has taken place as to whether these animals do great harm to trout water or not. The otter's defenders maintain that he really does little harm because he prefers eels to anything else. And they also argue that otters help to maintain a high standard of health among the trout by weeding out diseased and sickly fish. All this may sometimes be true. It may always be true. The trouble is that it is very difficult to prove. Once a water-bailiff has seen a few of his beloved trout lying dead on the bank, with shoulder-bites due to otters, he will certainly condemn them. But sadly enough the argument is now often academic, since in most places the lovely otter has become a very rare species.

Birds, however, can be even worse enemies. The heron, particularly, is a skilful and dangerous fisherman. He has one great stock-in-trade—immobility. For hours a heron will stand motionless in shallow water till a trout ventures near him, perhaps searching for food, perhaps returning to a spot he left in fright when the heron first arrived. Then a quick, deadly flash of the beak, which he can wield just like a dagger, and it is all over. Gulls and even kingfishers also eat trout. Some wild birds—like these—may only be legally shot if 'serious damage' to a fishery can be definitely proved. Others may be shot anyway, others never. A kingfisher's beauty, law apart, makes him inviolate. Few people could loose off a charge of shot at that colourful, gleaming little bird, whose presence is so often the delight of a day's fishing, even though early in the morning, when there are few witnesses about, he and his family take a few trout-fry.

Cormorants and shags take their toll of trout, too. So also do poaching cats. A friend of mine once owned a house near a trout farm to which a neighbouring cat had attached herself. This tabby showed a really remarkable capacity for intelligent reasoning. Every day the trout-fry in the ponds used to be fed at regular hours and they had found out that whenever food was thrown into the water it created a disturbance on the surface. They came to recognise this disturbance as a summons to their meals. Even a handful of earth thrown in would make them gather round hopefully.

The cat used to watch the feeding of the trout frequently, with an apparently dispassionate air. But one day, as my friend looked out of his bedroom window at sunrise, he saw her approaching one of the ponds. Delicately, she went up to the edge and patted the water with her paw, making a series of little splashes. Immediately the young trout gathered round waiting like Lewis Carroll's oysters to be fed, whereupon all she had to do was to scoop one out and retire into the bushes for breakfast.

Trout undoubtedly have a very long list of enemies against most of which only their speed of escape gives them any protection at all. It is therefore not in the least unnatural that they should be shy, nor that they should learn to be shy early. Trout-fry learn their lessons young and learn them quickly. Any shadow falling across the top of the water soon comes to be associated with a diving bird, while any unfamiliar shape moving along the bank can mean nothing but danger to them. But they also learn how to distinguish harmless animals from dangerous ones. If there are many cows in the meadows by the stream the trout will soon become quite accustomed to them, and they will also find out that they can live on friendly terms with ducks, coots and swans. Swans have an infuriating habit of swimming over rising trout just as you are beginning to fish for them. But the trout will not really be frightened if they know the swans well, or at any rate not for more than a minute or two. Soon they will be rising as eagerly as ever. Trout will sometimes feed practically under the necks of cows drinking in the river.

If the young trout survive, they go on adding to their weight year by year. The largest British trout known is the great Loch Awe fish, which weighed thirty-nine and a half pounds. He was caught in 1866 and then set up in a glass case. This was unfortunately destroyed by fire. Several other trout of over twenty pounds have been reliably reported, though the official record—as recognised by the British Record (Rod-caught) Fish Committee established in 1957—stands at a mere eighteen pounds and two ounces. This trout was caught in 1965, also in Scotland. But a great many trout in double figures have come from the big Irish lakes as well.

It may be surprising, but gigantic fish like these belong to exactly the same species as the little quarter-pounders we pull out of hill-streams. And they may not even be much older. They have simply fed better. They probably hatched in the little streams running into the big lakes, and grew there quite normally for some time, until one day they made their way down to the open water. There they found bigger and better food—such as the fry of other fish—and outstripped their brothers and sisters by twenty or thirty times.

By contrast, a trout is reputed to have lived in the bottom of a well for fifteen years. At the end of this time the trout was no heavier than a pound and a half, because there was not enough rich food. This was one example of how food is more important to the size of trout than age or heredity or any other single factor.

Rainbow trout stocked at a tender age may not grow to such a large size as brown trout—mainly because of their shorter life-span. They usually die at the end of their fourth year, but if they are lavishly fed in stewponds for some time before being stocked, they can reach really massive proportions—twenty pounds or even more.

Although brown trout live longer, most of them begin to go into a decline after six or seven years. For another year or two they may maintain their weight but each Spring they find it more and more difficult to get back into condition after spawning. Then they probably lose weight though they may still add an inch or two to their length. Their heads become large and ugly, their bodies lanky, their fins tattered, their skin discoloured. Their increasing weakness makes them worse and worse at hunting, and often blindness sets in as well, first in one eye, then in both.

You sometimes see these pathetic victims of old age in the streams, quite unaware of your approach, groping blindly among the weeds for food, hoping perhaps to smell it where they can no longer find it by sight. The best thing you can do for them is to shoot them or wire them or lift them out with a landing net.

Spawning always interrupts the growth of trout. They feed very little while they are occupied in breeding, so that it always takes them some time afterwards to replace the weight they have lost. On the whole, female trout tend to reach sexual maturity a year or two later than male trout and often grow larger in the end because of this fact. Male trout in hatcheries often spawn at the age of two. In natural conditions they may start at the same age—or they may wait till they are three or older. Once trout have spawned they usually spawn again in each successive year. Round about the end of September or beginning of October they move up towards the spawning-beds, which are always clean, well-oxygenated, gravelly shallows. This will probably be a pretty short journey if the river is well supplied with good spawning grounds, but if it is not the trout may travel a mile or more to find the right places. Once they have arrived there, they wait in the shallows for a week or two before they begin the actual process of spawning in late autumn or winter.

Before the female trout spawn, they excavate little 'nests' in the redds. They do this by performing violent bending and arching body-movements over the gravel. Although this is called 'cutting' they do not shift the gravel by physical contact with it, but by the currents of water which their body-movements create. Meanwhile the males are usually engaged in chasing each other or fighting among themselves—until one of them is attracted by the cutting activities of a female. Then he joins her and drives off other males.

When the nest is two or three inches deep, the female sheds her eggs in it and the male fertilises them with his milt, almost simultaneously. Immediately afterwards, the female moves just upstream and covers the eggs with gravel by beginning to cut her next nest. Each redd will consist of several nests and the trout, resting occasionally, may take several days to complete spawning. When it is over they drop slowly down-stream and leave the eggs to take care of themselves.

The time of year for spawning varies considerably from river to river. In some hill-streams the trout spawn in October, while in the chalk-streams spawning trout have been seen as late as February. The temperature of the water may influence trout here. Trout eggs hatch in thirty-eight days at a temperature of fifty-two degrees Fahrenheit but they take a hundred days at a temperature only ten degrees lower. The trout of hill-streams may have learned to compensate for colder water by spawning a little earlier.

The fate of the eggs is often rather a sad one—for many of them come to grief. Trout lay about eight hundred eggs for every pound of their weight. Some will be unfertilised. Others may be choked by silt. The trout inside an egg needs oxygen and the skin of the egg allows oxygen to pass through, but not if silt is deposited on top. Other eggs, again, may be eaten by water-animals, so that the mortality at this stage is huge, practically impossible to estimate. A trout's chances of staying alive become increasingly better as he grows older; but just two trout eggs in a thousand, at a very optimistic guess, produce mature trout.

When trout have finished spawning they soon begin feeding again to get back their weight and strength. The early spawners and the smaller fish regain their condition soonest, provided that there is an abundant food supply. In some waters they are in fine fettle again by March, ready for an early start to the fishing season. But in Hampshire, because the trout are never really in fighting condition until April and sometimes not till May, the first day of the season has to be postponed till then. It is always a shame to take out thin, half-hearted fish before they can put up such a good resistance or make such a good meal as they might. The heavier fish always take longer to recover, as they have more bulk to build up.

Once they have started, trout go on feeding all summer, all autumn and even into winter. They are less hungry in the hottest months of the year than they were in the Spring, but in September and October they sometimes feed greedily again, perhaps to prepare for the lean time of spawning. There is a widespread idea that trout are rather pernickety about their fare. In reality, however, they will eat almost anything. Within the bounds of being carnivorous, trout are virtually omnivorous and they have been caught on unlikely things like mice. The same trout's stomach, when you have caught him on a Mayfly, may also contain beetles, tadpoles, worms, minnows, shrimps, snails and enough little animals of other sorts to start a small zoo.

All these will have been eaten during the last nineteen hours or so, which is roughly the time it takes a trout's digestion to work. The reason why he is often so very difficult to catch is that at any one particular moment he may be devoting himself exclusively to only

1. SUCCESS for a keen dry-fly fisherwoman. Shown here on the Test is Mrs Lucy Havelock-Allan with an enviable rainbow. Nick Mitchell, by her side, has just netted the fish for her. Catching a trophy trout can bring an extra bonus to any flyfisher. With this particular ambition fulfilled, he or she may well begin to feel that sheer size is no longer so important as it seemed before. Smaller fish will be less disappointing and soon the satisfaction of catching a really difficult trout, instead of simply a large one, will be likely to reign supreme.

2. THE BEST LANDING NET, in the author's opinion, is one with a collapsible head, a telescopic handle and a solid circular frame. The collapsible head makes for easy carrying while the telescopic handle helps to land fish from high banks. The solid circular frame, unlike many triangular frames, never tangles and also allows the net to be used to root around in a weed-bed for a trout taking refuge there. Be sure that the net is always very accessible. The accomplished fisherman in the picture is well aware of all this. He is Ted Hughes, the Poet Laureate, photographed on the Itchen.

3. THE WORST MISTAKE possible while landing a trout is to swoop or scoop at him with the net. The result will all too probably be as shown in this photograph of an incident on the Test. A desperate swoop has failed to get the trout into the net. But the rim of the net has managed to throw the trout into mid-air, where almost certainly the leader will break or the hook lose its hold. The correct way to land any trout can be seen in the photo below.

4. THE SAFEST WAY to land a trout is to sink the net in the water, to draw the trout gently over it, and finally to lift up the net with the trout inside. When a fish is netted from the bank it is usually wise to kneel down since a trout often makes a few frenzied last-minute struggles if he catches sight of a figure looming over him. The photograph here is of Sir Michael Hordern – the distinguished actor and a highly distinguished fisherman as well – landing a trout perfectly on the Wiltshire Avon.

3

4

one sort of food. You can seldom catch a trout rising to flies on a minnow, or a shrimping trout on a fly. The trout's willingness to come up to the surface for flies—and this obviously includes the fisherman's dry fly—depends on whether he is accustomed to feeding on flies, and on whether any of those flies are actually hatching at the time.

Dry-fly water

Different types of lake, reservoir or stream produce different qualities of dry-fly fishing. Rivers, to start with, fall broadly speaking into four categories—sluggish, gentle, fastish and very fast—and each category has its own structure of animal life to influence the trout's behaviour.

First, sluggish rivers. These are the ones that flow so slowly that silt has been deposited on their beds in a thick carpet. Weeds find it easy to grow and there will be plenty of algae in the weeds. On the other hand the slowness of the water does not make for good oxygenation and the weeds take up a large amount of oxygen by night. Trout will not live here in very great numbers, nor will many of the flies most important to a dry-fly fisherman. March Browns, Dark and Medium Olives, and Iron Blues, to mention only four, all need plenty of oxygen passing over their bodies to allow them to breathe.

Most of the food in sluggish rivers, therefore, will consist of snails, beetles, worms and other animals only found well underneath the water. There will be a good many coarse fish to feed on them, and such trout as there are will feed on them, too. Or, if they are big enough, they may feed on the smaller coarse fish as Thames trout do. Fly-life will be fairly limited—and will be made up mainly of Mayflies, midges and some caddis-flies. You may have some sport, and even catch very large fish when these flies put in an appearance, but on the whole there are not many trout in sluggish rivers and they are not regular surface feeders.

Next, there are rivers that flow gently but not sluggishly, depositing silt only in certain places, and where the current is fast enough to keep areas of gravel or chalk bright and clean. These rivers, particularly if the water contains plenty of dissolved salts, may be the best of all. Good weeds—to provide cover and food for fly-larvae—

will grow in both the gravel and the silt and there should be ample oxygen for both trout and insects. Invading coarse fish will not like it as much as the slower rivers and most river-flies will flourish there, showing themselves in a daily hatch sufficient to bring the trout up to the surface. As well as flies, you will find shrimps, snails, worms and all sorts of other nourishment for trout. There may even be crayfish. Crayfish need alkaline water and oxygen, and wherever they thrive the trout seem to grow big quickly. A fish has to reach a weight of about a pound and a quarter before he takes any real interest in these crustaceans—the largest in fresh water—but when he begins feeding on them he may even double his weight in a single year. So these gentle streams sometimes provide excellent dry-fly fishing, with plenty of large trout, most of whom may be frequent surface-feeders.

Then there are the slightly faster streams. If they flow fairly quickly over gravel but still have quite a few protected places where weeds can get a foothold, your fishing should still be good. As the stream runs faster and faster, and weed-beds thin out, you will find fewer and fewer Mayflies, Olives and Iron Blues, but their scarcity is often offset by rather more Stoneflies, March Browns and other flies. There will be a fair number of the caddis-flies who live in gravel, but not many shrimps or snails outside the few weed-beds. Trout food will become generally less plentiful as the weed-beds disappear, but even where the stream hastens and bubbles over rocks, moss can grow precariously on the stones and boulders to afford cover for insects, so that much of the available food continues to consist of flies, rather than of bottom-food. Oxygen is no problem. So on these faster streams, provided they are clear and unpolluted, you will usually find plenty of trout prepared to feed on the surface. They are unlikely to be nearly so large as chalk-stream trout and there will be fewer big hatches of fly, especially during mid-summer. But simply because of the comparative shortage of food, the trout will probably be hungry for a lot of the time and if you know where to find them, you can often bring them up by throwing a dry fly over them.

When the stream is so swift that it nearly always creates a turbulence on the top of the water, it is likely to be better for the wet fly than a dry fly. There is no point whatsoever in sticking religiously to the dry fly when a sunk fly is more successful. Even on these streams, however, a dry fly can be more profitable than a wet fly at certain times, especially in high summer when the water is low and very clear. Apart from stagnant or polluted rivers, where there is no oxygen, the only ones that will support hardly any trout are those with beds of sand. A trout would have an exceedingly lean time of it there, because although weeds can consolidate themselves in silt and gravel, and moss or algae can cling to stones and boulders, shifting sand offers absolutely no anchorage for plants. And where there are no plants, there are seldom any small animals and insects for trout to eat.

Before leaving the rivers, it is worth noticing that there is an important difference between rain-fed and spring-fed streams. Those that are rain-fed, where the surface water from the ground runs directly into the river, are always subject to floods or spates. During a spate, fish and other large animals can take refuge from the pace of the torrent behind stones or in the quieter backwaters, but small animals like insects are often swept away and die. Droughts are another trouble, since insect-eggs and larvae may again be destroyed through being left high and dry by the falling water. Spring-fed streams—such as you find in many chalk districts—do not suffer from the same trouble. Here, the rain seldom rushes straight downhill to swell the river, but filters gradually through the chalk, reappearing in the springs weeks or even months later. The chalk acts, in fact, as a sort of reservoir, keeping the level of the water steady, guarding against spates and droughts equally. The trout-food is usually safer as a result, and one further advantage, from the fisherman's point of view, is that the river is all the less likely to get high and coloured. A tropical shower may make life unpleasant for him, but unless it lasts a long time it will not make fishing impossible by sending the river down looking like cocoa.

Finally, still water. The main difference between still water and flowing water, as regards trout-food, is the presence of zooplankton in still water. Zooplankton consists of minute free-floating organisms which live in lakes and reservoirs—otherwise they are carried away by the current—and most trout except the largest feed on them at times. They are very tiny creatures and seldom build big trout, although the whalebone whale—the largest animal that the Earth has ever known—does keep up his terrific bulk on their salt-water relatives. Trout in certain Swiss lakes reach a weight of two pounds, feeding on nothing but plankton.

Reservoirs and lakes often contain a large proportion of bottom food and mid-water food. Some of it—such as shrimp and coarse-fish fry—will go to nourish big trout. Sticklebacks (which can be imitated by certain still-water 'lures') are also eaten in quantity. The balance of the trout's food, therefore, tends to weigh rather heavily against the fish being likely to rise very frequently. Wet flies and nymphs and 'attractors' lures are usually better bets than any dry fly. But on some natural lakes, notably the great lakes of Ireland, there are excellent hatches of Mayfly. And on most reservoirs and lakes Sedges (or Caddis flies) and midges will hatch in the evening. Nor is that the end of it. Many still waters contain other flies as well—such as the Pond Olive. Shallow lakes are on the whole better for still-water flies than deep ones, because the larvae cannot live and grow where the light never penetrates. A number of still-water flies prefer rich, alkaline water, which rather limits their distribution, but wherever they abound there may be good hatches of fly to induce the trout to feed on the surface—at times. Then the dry fly works.

To sum up, good dry-fly water can best be described as a river, reservoir or lake where the trout come up to the surface nearly every day to feed on hatches of fly. On any other water, the best fisherman is the one who suits his method to the weather, the time of the year and the behaviour of the trout on the day he goes fishing. The wet-fly fisherman has every right to look down his nose at a hide-bound dry-fly fisherman who waits all day for a fish to rise where there are no flies to hatch, or who fishes his fly on the surface of the water when the trout are feeding well beneath it. The worm fisherman, too, can afford to laugh at a man dry-fly fishing in a spate, because then the trout will be gorging themselves on worms and grubs washed down by the high water. The dry fly has its time and place on many rivers and still waters—not all—and dry-fly fishermen use it there, not because it makes them feel superior to wet-fly fishermen, but simply because it is more successful.

— CHAPTER 6 —

Natural Flies

Is it really necessary for a fisherman to be able to tell which species of fly is hatching? Must he also imitate it exactly? Some fishermen—who have been dubbed purists—say that he must. But others go so far as to say 'any fly's the same as the next to a trout'. Another school, which believes in good casting, will tell you: 'It's not the fly, but the driver'. And there are still other fishermen who believe in steady, persistent fishing and say: 'The only successful fly is the one that's always on the water'. How very confusing! The truth is—of course—that everyone is perfectly right. Any fly will catch fish—at some times, and in some places. Good casting is a tremendous help at any time, and in any place. Persistent fishermen often catch trout when more skilful ones have packed up in despair. And, to give the purists their due, trout can sometimes be very choosy indeed.

The choosiest trout of all probably live in the chalk-streams. Occasionally they will only accept one sort of fly. But even on less heavily fished waters a fisherman who is also a bit of an amateur entomologist usually stands a better chance, even if it is sometimes only a slightly better chance, of catching trout than if he knew nothing at all about flies. And he has one further asset, which the purists sometimes do not admit to. He gets more sheer fun. Identifying living creatures is a fascinating hobby in its own right. Ask any bird-watcher. Fishermen must be rather like bird-watchers in this way.

Entomologists often call insects by their Latin names. This is not nearly so silly as it sounds. The trouble with the English names of flies is that there are so many of them for each sort of fly. For instance it would be quite possible for four fishermen to have an argument at the end of the day as to whether the flies on the water had been Dark

Olives or Blue Duns or Spring Olives or Whirling Duns, and none of them might realize that they were all talking of the same fly. The Latin name for it is *Baëtis rhodani* and this is the only Latin name for it wherever it hatches, in any country. Latin names do avoid mixing flies up.

So I shall make no apology for mentioning the proper Latin names here. They may help to serve as a reference, even if you do not remember them. The flies which are most important to fishermen, because they are the most common as trout-food, can be divided into four main types—or 'orders', to use the right scientific word. Let me now sketch very briefly the characteristics and life-histories of these four 'orders'. Later on, in other chapters, I shall try to describe some of the individual flies more closely.

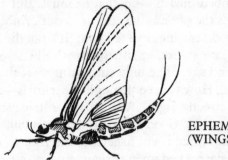

EPHEMEROPTERAN DUN
(WINGS UPRIGHT)

Here are the names of the four orders. First, the *Ephemeroptera*—or up-winged flies. Second, the *Trichoptera*—or sedge-flies. (These are sometimes also described as caddis-flies.) Third, the *Plecoptera* or stone-flies. And last, the *Diptera*—which include Gnats, Midges, Smuts and ordinary Bluebottles. There are a great many different flies within these four types, some of them common and some of them rare.

Most fishermen rely on the *Ephemeroptera* for the bulk of their sport. Mayflies, Olives and Iron Blues are all *Ephemeroptera* and when they hatch out they all have four wings which point up towards the sky like the sail of a boat. The front pair of wings is very large, usually slightly longer than the body of the fly itself, while the second pair is much smaller and very difficult to see since it is almost hidden by the first pair. No other flies carry their wings in an upright fashion and it is lucky that the Ephemeropterans do. Their high wings make them much easier to spot on the water than any other sort of fly.

All the Ephemeropterans pass through four separate stages of development. Although they are called flies they can only fly for a very short period at the end of their lives. They start off as eggs, below the surface of the water. After a little time, which is usually a few weeks, these small eggs hatch out into nymphs—little grub-like creatures which still get their oxygen from the water and not from the air. The nymphal stage is by far the longest in the fly's existence. Most of them spend six months to one year as nymphs and Mayflies may even live in this form for two whole years.

If you buy a cheap muslin net at the village store, the sort of net that small children use for catching minnows, and then work it around in the weeds of a chalk stream, it will come up with plenty of wriggling nymphs in it. On them depends the future sport that the stream will offer. They will vary in size and colour, since they will be the nymphs of various different flies at various ages. All of them, however, will represent those particular flies that like living in the weeds in running water. Not all nymphs do, and their separate preferences mean that you find different sorts of fly in different sorts of water.

Here are some of the preferences. All *Baëtis* nymphs like living in rivers and streams rather than in lakes. The genus *Baëtis* is a very large one within the *Ephemeroptera*, including the Dark Olive, the Medium Olive, the Iron Blue and two Pale Wateries. The nymphs of these flies, like many river-bred species, need water flowing past their bodies before they can absorb oxygen through their body walls. That is why the nymphs in the muslin net will very soon die if they are kept in a jam-jar. It is not so much the fact that there is too little oxygen in the jam-jar, but that the nymphs cannot make use of it unless the water is actually moving.

These nymphs are swimming nymphs. They are streamlined in shape, can dart quickly for a short distance and can make their way from weed to weed or stone to stone. Most of them can exist in either acid or alkaline water, though some occur rather more commonly in alkaline rivers such as the chalk streams. Apart from the *Baëtis* flies are one or two other swimming nymphs that exist only in rivers and there is one common still-water swimming nymph, the nymph of the Pond Olive (*Cloëon dipterum*). This nymph also absorbs oxygen through its body wall, but it flaps its gills in order to keep water moving past it. It creates its own little current, in fact, so as to be able to breathe. One Pale Watery—the Small Spurwing, or *Centroptilum luteolum*—has a remarkably adaptable swimming nymph. It can breathe equally well in slow rivers, fast streams and lakes, so it is one of the commonest and most widespread flies in the country.

NYMPH
(of a typical Ephemeropteran)

Other nymphs, which prefer other places, hardly swim at all but crawl slowly around the bottom of rivers and lakes. They usually have thicker bodies and stiff, strong legs to help them. Probably the best-known, at any rate to fishermen, is the Blue-winged Olive—*Ephemerella ignita*—which will make its home in almost any flowing water, acid or alkaline, and is the most likely fly to hatch in the evening on many rivers. Then there is the Claret Dun—*Leptophlebia vespertina*. This nymph can live in lakes, ponds or streams but it seems to prefer acid peaty water to alkaline water, which is a very rare liking for flies to have. Another set of crawling nymphs is made up by the four species of *Caenis*, the Fisherman's Curse, the smallest of the Ephemeropterans and terribly difficult to imitate when it is on the water.

Other nymphs again cling tenaciously to rocks and stones and have developed flattened bodies so as to give themselves a firm grip. The March Brown—*Rhithrogena haarupi*—is a perfect example. It not only has a flat body, offering very little resistance to the current, but is also uses a suction arrangement, whereby it can make a vacuum between itself and a rock and so avoid being swept away even by the fastest streams. The March Brown is a river-dweller but the Yellow May Dun and August Dun—*Heptagenia sulphurea* and *Ecdyonurus dispar*—can both be found in rocky lakes as well. Both nymphs are flattened and can live in either fast or still water so long as it is not too acid and has the rocks and stones which they like.

The only nymphs that do not swim, crawl or cling are the Mayfly nymphs. They dig and burrow. Just as moles and badgers have developed strong forelegs for excavation purposes, so have Mayflies. They dig out little tunnels in the silt or mud of rivers and lakes and set up house in them. Like all flies which are capable of living in still water they can make their own current by using their gills.

So different waters contain different kinds of nymphs. They are usually vegetarians and feed mainly on the algae covering under-water plants or stones, and sometimes also on decaying plants at the bottom of the water. Their natural enemies are many and they have to beware of nearly any creature larger than themselves. Even tiny water mites eat the very young nymphs, while older nymphs make good meals for the larvae of dragonflies and stoneflies, as well as water spiders and—of course—fish.

Over a period the nymphs grow steadily. Every so often they moult and shed a complete outer case to make room for their increasing size. Inside each successive case the wings of the flies, non-existent when the nymphs first hatched from the egg, gradually take shape. Slowly the nymphs begin to look more and more like wingless versions of adult flies, until one day the time comes for them to hatch.

If fishermen could prophesy exactly when flies of a particular sort would choose to hatch, there would be a lot less time wasted by the riverbank. But nobody can. Water-temperature, air-temperature, atmospheric pressure and sunshine must all have something to do with it. Different flies seem to prefer different conditions. Iron Blues, for instance, nearly always hatch best in cold weather and Blue-winged Olives nearly always hatch best in the evening. But exceptions do occur and no-one, with all the thermometers and barometers in the world, has ever been able to guarantee that a hatch of so-and-so will take place between the hours of such-and-such.

When a quantity of flies of the same species decide to leave the water and take to the air, this is a fisherman's hatch. It should bring trout onto the feed. A few flies may hatch singly beforehand and afterwards but most of them are guided by some mass-instinct and choose roughly the same time. All over the river, or all over the lake, flies appear at the same moment as if summoned by a rallying-cry.

The nymphs hatch in different ways. Some species of fly climb out of their final nymphal cases below the surface, and then come up to the air surrounded by a film of gas to keep them dry. Other crawl out onto a stone or reed before they change from nymph to fly. But the majority of Ephemeropterans swim or float to the surface and hatch there. These mature nymphs usually have some air inside their skins to help them ascend and how it gets there is something of a mystery. Some swimming nymphs may pay a visit to the surface and swallow a gulp of air a little time before hatching, others may obtain it from dissolved gases in the water, and others by sucking it from the stems of reeds.

Once at the surface a nymph splits its case down the back and the adult fly struggles out. The crumpled wings, imprisoned for so long, soon expand in the warm air and after a flutter or two the insect is able to fly clumsily and laboriously towards the shore. The nymphal 'shuck' is left behind. Now the fly has entered the third stage of its life—that of a sub-imago, or dun. It no longer absorbs oxygen from the water through its body-walls, since the shedding of its case has revealed a series of very tiny air-holes underneath. Air filters in through these and oxygen is extracted from it.

A dun cannot eat or drink. Its mouth-parts are useless. This is one of the reasons why the lives of Ephemeropterans above the surface are so pathetically short. When they have hatched they take shelter in the neighbouring foliage, often on the undersides of leaves, and wait for their next and last transformation. If you search under the leaves by the side of a river you can nearly always find several sorts of duns sitting, resting and waiting. The time varies. Species of *Caenis* sometimes only spend a few minutes as duns before going into their fourth stage, Mayflies may take a few days, but most flies take about twenty-four hours or a little longer if the weather is cold.

Ephemeropterans are the only flies that change at all after becoming winged. The change consists of a further moult, when they shed one more complete skin, the whole outer covering of head, body, wings and tails. If you keep some duns in a jam-jar or butterfly cage you can watch them do it, and it is amazing to find that so delicate an insect can take off another entire coat. The fly that emerges is a 'perfect' fly—an imago—and is even more delicate than the dun. The colour of its body is sharper and brighter, its wings are more transparent and its tails and feelers are thinner and longer. It may have two tails or three tails. All Ephemeropteran nymphs possess three short tails, but when the fly eventually hatches it usually only has two longer ones. Some species, however, such as Mayflies and Blue-winged Olives, have three.

As soon as flies commence the last stage of their lives fishermen call them spinners. Again they wait under cover for a while, until the time comes for them to mate, and during this period their colours tend to alter slightly. The fly that finally mates may not look quite the same as a younger spinner and may bear practically no resemblance at all to the dun, except in size. A male Iron Blue Dun, for instance, is a dark steel-blue colour all over, while its spinner—the Jenny Spinner—is nearly all white except for a touch of dark-brown at the end of its body. All this is fascinating to watch but it makes the recognition of flies rather more difficult.

When the flies are ready to mate, and when weather conditions are right, they fly out from their shelter. Usually they choose fairly calm weather, or if the weather is windy they find protected places behind woods or bushes. The males and females have to meet each other. They do this by dancing. The males collect in swarms, sometimes of only a few flies and sometimes of thousands, and perform an aerial dance during which the swarm keeps roughly in the same spot unless it is swept away by a sudden breeze. The dance of most species consists of soaring up a few feet, then dipping down again, then soaring up again, and continuing like this for perhaps as long as several hours. Some species hover and do not really dance, but this is not so common and the very name spinner comes from the endless rising and falling of the dancing flies.

The females come upon these swarms and fly round the fringes of them until they can attract a male, or several males. The males then leave the swarm, pursue the female, and the successful suitor mates with her in mid-air. He has a tiny pair of forceps right at the end of his body with which he can hold her. Male spinners usually have a different colouring from female spinners of the same species, but often the presence of these forceps is the easiest way of telling a male dun from a female dun when they first hatch.

After mating the two flies sink down on to the ground, still joined firmly together. Soon they separate. They have not much longer left to live. The male may go back to join his swarm for a short time but he dies a little later. The female may take shelter again for several hours, or she may not. Then she flies off to lay her eggs.

Species of *Baëtis* crawl underneath the water, down a weed or rock or anything sticking up above the surface, in order to lay eggs. As they submerge a film of air sticks to their bodies to keep them dry. They normally lay their eggs on stones, where they are held by a gluey substance which covers them. Afterwards the spinners crawl or float to the surface, helped by the envelope of air. Some of the little creatures may then perish immediately and if not they are likely to die within a very few minutes.

Spinners of other species lay their eggs on the surface. Some of them sit on the water to do so, some release their eggs from the air and some dip briefly down on to the surface to let the water wash the eggs away from their bodies. The number of eggs laid by these spinners may be anything from a few hundred to several thousand according to the species. When they have finished their job of egg-laying nearly all the female spinners die exhausted on the surface of the water. They are then described as 'spent' flies.

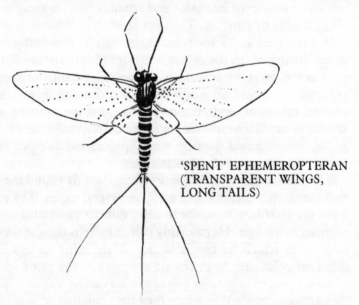

'SPENT' EPHEMEROPTERAN
(TRANSPARENT WINGS,
LONG TAILS)

Trout have a chance to feed on Ephemeropterans at any stage after they have hatched from the egg. They sometimes hunt among the weed-beds for nymphs. Any nymph that temporarily leaves its hiding place is in danger of being snapped up. Perhaps the most dangerous time of all for nymphs is when they make the ascent to the surface just before hatching, because then they have no cover and are easy meat for fish to catch. And even afterwards their troubles are hardly over. Trout will usually be ready and waiting to rise and take them while they hatch. Birds will swoop down to pluck duns neatly from the water. The same birds may take them in the air before they can reach shelter, and again later on while they are dancing as spinners. Finally the trout can feed on the spent flies as they lie dead or dying on the surface.

Fishermen have almost as many chances to catch trout as trout have to catch flies. If the trout are feeding on nymphs below the surface, a fisherman can catch them on a sunken imitation of a nymph. If they are rising to a hatch of duns, he can catch them on an artificial dun, and when there is a fall of spinners he can use an artificial spinner. Occasionally trout feeding on a fly at one particular stage will refuse it at all other stages. So it is sometimes far more important to realize whether the fish are taking nymphs, duns or spinners than to recognize the exact species.

The Ephemeropterans are the mainstay of most dry-fly waters. Other types of fly, however, can be very useful too, and among them are the *Trichoptera*. The *Trichoptera*—usually called sedge-flies or caddis-flies—are quite easy to distinguish from *Ephemeroptera* because they never carry their wings upright but fold them back over their bodies like the roof of a house. The shape of a typical sedge-fly is shown in the picture below. There are nearly two hundred species of them in the British Isles, though only a few of these are of real interest to fishermen.

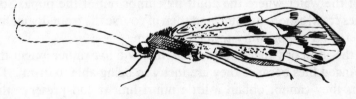

SEDGE FLY
(HUMPED WINGS)

These sedge-flies also develop in four stages but unlike Ephemeropterans they go through three underwater stages and only one winged stage. The larvae, which correspond to the nymphs of up-winged flies, hatch from the eggs and live among the stones and plants of rivers and lakes. Many of them build themselves cases of sand, gravel, wood, leaves or whatever materials happen to be available. The cases give them some protection from attack and also provide excellent camouflage. Other species of sedge-fly, however, do not build cases but live naked. While they grow the larvae feed not only on vegetable matter but on small water animals and on the eggs of other insects as well. They are voracious creatures and so can cause a lot of harm amongst the eggs and young nymphs of the up-winged flies.

After a little while the larvae go into a quiescent stage of pupation. Each fly forms a pupa either inside its case or in a silk cocoon which it spins for itself. Then it ceases eating and hardly moves until it hatches. When that time comes, which may be after several weeks or

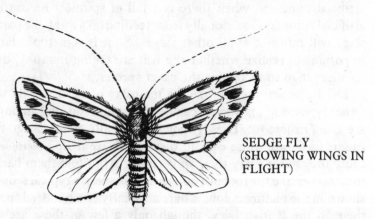

SEDGE FLY
(SHOWING WINGS IN
FLIGHT)

several months, it tears open its case or cocoon and swims up to the top of the water where the adult fly climbs out of the pupa. Some species crawl ashore to hatch and then of course the trout do not have such a good opportunity to feed on them.

In the adult or winged stage sedge-flies will live rather longer than up-winged flies because they are lucky in being able to drink. This means they cannot obtain a little nourishment and preserve their body-moisture. After perhaps a week or a fortnight the males and the females will find each other. The flies then mate at rest instead of in the air. Finally the females fly off to lay their eggs either on the surface or by crawling beneath it, and often float spent and dead on the water after this is done.

Certain species of sedge-flies, such as Grannoms and Grey Flags, only live in flowing water while others are equally comfortable in rivers or lakes. Their complete life-cycle may take one, two or three years. Trout feed on both the larvae and the pupae but these are rather difficult for a dry-fly fisherman to imitate. The hatching flies, the egg-laying flies and the spent flies all provide very good sport, however, and they have an extra advantage in that they sometimes stay on the water very late, long after other sorts of fly have vanished. On the chalk streams, for instance, there is usually an evening hatch of Blue-winged Olives during the summer, and when this stops at dusk you can often catch trout for another twenty minutes or so on a sedge.

Stone-flies—the *Plecoptera*—look superficially not unlike sedge-flies, since they also fold their wings back. But they do not hump

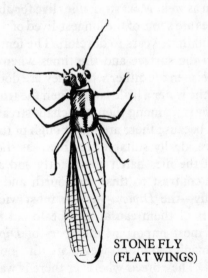

STONE FLY
(FLAT WINGS)

their wings over themselves like a sloping roof, as the sedge-flies do. Most of them carry their wings quite flat, more like a level roof, while a few fold them closely round their bodies like a skin-tight garment. The wings of all stone-flies fit much more tightly than those of caddis-flies.

Nearly any type of water will support a number of stone-flies of various sorts but they are only really common in stony or gravelly river-courses or in lakes with stony edges. They vary in size considerably. The Large Stone-fly grows to well over an inch in length, while the Needle-fly, the smallest of the stone-flies, is only about a third as long.

Although the up-winged flies and sedge-flies have four stages of development, the stone-flies have just three—egg stage, nymph stage and eventually winged stage. The nymphs or larvae, when they come out of the eggs, crawl on the bottom among the stones and feed on the larger plants as well as on algae. The bigger species of stone-fly eat small animals. When the time comes all the nymphs crawl along the bottom, up the shore and onto dry land before hatching, a habit which means that trout can never take them on or near the surface as they can other nymphs.

The flies do not mate and lay their eggs until after two or three weeks. Like the sedge-flies they can drink and some species can even eat vegetation as well. Most stone-flies live for about a year in all. The very large ones are some of the longest-lived of water insects, because they take a full three years to develop. The females of all species lay their eggs on the surface and the times when stone-flies are most useful to fishermen are either while they are doing this or while they are dying on the water a little later. Then the trout may rise to them.

In many waters, among them the chalk streams, stone-flies are of no real value because there are not enough of them. It is only where conditions are ideally suitable for them, as they are in rocky hill-streams, that the flies hatch abundantly and are worth imitating. But in strict contrast to this, the fourth and last major order of fisherman's fly—the *Diptera*—is the most wide-spread of all and large numbers of them can always be found in any still water or stream. The most important members of *Diptera*, from the still-water fisherman's point of view, are the non-biting Midges or *Chironomidae*. They breed wherever there is water of any sort, even in the water of drinking-troughs, rain-butts and ditches.

There are usually plenty of Chironomids—or Midges—in ponds, lakes and reservoirs everywhere. They are long-legged insects—the length of their legs is a helpful distinguishing feature—with pale wings a little shorter than their bodies. Many of them are a bit longer than the misleading name midge might lead you to suppose, and there are some species which reach a size of half an inch. They go through four stages—egg, larva, pupa, fly. The larvae are worm-like, without obvious limbs. Some of them are pale-olive in colour; others,

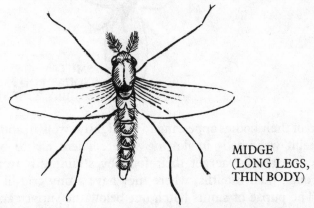

MIDGE
(LONG LEGS,
THIN BODY)

frequently called blood-worms, are bright red in colour and can live on far less oxygen than any other water insect. In badly polluted water these blood-worms are often the only insects that flourish.

Whether the water is still or flowing, deep or shallow, acid or alkaline, midges of one species or another will be able to make it their home. A good many of the larvae like burying themselves in mud but others can be found almost anywhere. Some live only for weeks, others longer. The larvae pupate and the pupae swim up to the top of the water to hatch. The trout feed on the hatching pupae—which can be imitated—and sometimes rise also to the female flies when they lay their eggs on the surface.

The Chironomids are extremely useful on still waters, where there are less flies of other sorts than in most rivers. In rivers, however, they will be augmented and perhaps outnumbered by the *Simulium*—or Reed-Smut—group of *Diptera*. Smuts, which breed in almost any flowing water, are very small, thick, stumpy flies with dark bodies and light wings which they carry in the same way as a housefly. Unlike the midges their legs are short. Fishermen call the slightly larger species Black Gnats and although the true Black Gnats—such as the species *Bibio johannis*—belong to a different group of *Diptera* and breed on land, they all look much alike and the same artificial fly serves to imitate them.

Smuts again pass from egg to larva to pupa to fly. They also live for varying periods. The larvae are little, pale, thin creatures, with one

SMUT
(SQUAT BODY,
STUBBY WINGS)

end of their bodies appearing to be slightly swollen, and they usually inhabit weed-beds in flowing water. There has to be a current, because the larvae get their food by straining it from the water through their mouths, where they have a tiny grid-like filter.

The pupae of smuts hatch out below the surface and the adults float up to the top completely enclosed in a bubble of gas so that they can fly away quite dry. They may be taken by trout at this stage, but the fish seem fonder of them when they are lying spent on the stream after laying their eggs.

That ends the list of the types of fly that are most interesting to a fisherman. The number of different species often sounds a little alarming at first. But the great thing is—as Part III tries to explain—that the variety of flies likely to hatch at any one time, on any one day, in any one place can be narrowed down to a very few, and it is usually possible to recognise these fairly quickly. There is luckily no need for a fisherman to carry a trunkful of flies—most of us clutter our flyboxes unnecessarily—nor need he keep a Latin dictionary.

PART THREE

Chalk Streams and Other Waters

CHAPTER 7

Early Season

All through the winter, and even in early Spring, a river looks unfriendly—secretive—discouraging. You do not feel welcome there. Probably the colourful beauty of the valley around it has stayed in your memory long after your rod has been packed up at the end of September; but now, at the beginning of March, there is little promise of colour in the bleakness of the countryside. The bright, golden days of the previous summer seem a long way off, and you wonder if they will ever come again.

Even the chalk streams, crystal-clear before, are sullen and swollen from the autumn and winter rainfall. They swirl along through drab meadows. If you peer into them you may not be able to see the river-bed except in the shallows. Even if you can, there are no trout to be seen and you begin to wonder whether there are any fish in the water at all. Perhaps it was over-fished last year? Perhaps some form of disease or pollution has killed the trout or sent them elsewhere?

The stream is depressingly bare of weed as well. There is not much left to remind you of those rich, food-producing beds of ranunculus and starwort that you cut with so much labour only a few months ago.

But even now, in rivers, streams and lakes all over the country, life is still carrying on below the surface. Tiny nymphs are growing steadily—not so fast as they will when the water temperature rises, but growing all the same—and getting closer to the time when they will hatch out. The trout have finished spawning and are waiting for food in their various hiding places. Heaven knows exactly where they hide themselves. When there is no food about, it is possible to walk along stretches of water that look as if they could not conceal a minnow, and never see a trout. Yet you know the fish are somewhere there. Then, when the flies come onto the scene, you can look again and see four—five—six—seven trout all rising merrily.

At the moment, however, both trout and nymphs are waiting for more sun to bring out more water-food. Then the river will suddenly wake up. The sun will make the weed grow, the weed will collect algae, the algae will provide food for the nymphs, the nymphs will become strong and active, and as soon as they hatch the trout will feed on them greedily to make up the weight they have lost in spawning.

You may see a few Large Dark Olives hatching out on the chalk-streams in early March, with perhaps an odd trout splashing up to take them. They will not necessarily hatch best on the sunniest days. But only the sun can speed up the tempo of underwater life. In winter the tempo is rather slow and it must quicken before fishing can begin.

By mid-March, although there may be more insect-life about, the trout in the chalk streams will still be recovering from spawning. They will be very thin. It is a shame to fish for skeletons when a few weeks will put flesh on them, so chalk-stream fishermen must wait till later on before starting the season.

Many other rivers and streams, however, open for trout-fishing on either March 1st or March 15th, and the trout in them are far plumper by that time. Some of them have wonderful hatches of March Brown, an early fly seldom found on any chalk stream. Perhaps the Usk is the first really famous British river to come into condition, and here the March Brown will be in full swing during the last half of March and the beginning of April.

The March Brown can hardly be mistaken for anything else. It is a big, brownish up-winged fly. It has buff wings and a rather unpronounceable Latin name like a hiccup—*Rhithrogena haarupi*. If you forget the Mayfly, the March Brown is a very large fly for an Ephemeropteran, and it hatches incredibly suddenly. You may be staring at a blank stretch of water, where not a trout is rising. Then, a minute later, the air seems to be filled with clumsy dull-coloured insects, all fluttering on their way from the water to the shore.

The only trouble with the March Browns is that they often stop hatching almost as suddenly as they start. Sometimes they only go on for about a quarter of an hour. So you have to make the most of them.

This will hardly be the time for excessive caution. The trout, as early in the year as this, will be greedy and forgetful of the various dangers they learned about last summer. The best course is to tie on a March Brown quickly, cover as many fish as possible in the brief period of excitement and land as many as possible without delay.

When the fly stops hatching the river seems dead again. But there may be another hatch after a short time. In fact, there may be as many as three or four hatches of March Browns during the day, probably between eleven o'clock in the morning and three o'clock in the afternoon. If there are not, casting a dry fly into likely places may always bring up a fish or two. But a wet fly will probably be more successful. At the very beginning of the season, the trout are not really used to feeding on the surface, except on the March Brown. Some other flies may hatch but usually not very many. For most of the day, therefore, the trout are more likely to be looking for nymphs and grubs rather deeper in the water. So a wet fly reaches them better and can account for trout before, between and after hatches of March Brown.

When April comes, the chalk-stream season begins—though many chalk-stream fishermen wait till May—and it begins with the Large Dark Olive. This Olive is not quite so big as the March Brown, but it is another pretty sizeable fly. It appears on a great many rivers, not only on chalk streams, and has a dark olive-green body with dull bluey-grey wings. Among other names given to *Baëtis rhodani* in various parts of the country are Dark Olive, Large Spring Olive and Winter Olive. It is easily the most frequent fly on the chalk streams at the beginning of April.

The most probable time of day for the Large Dark Olives to hatch is about one o'clock, but they may appear as early as eleven if the weather is warm and sunny, or as late as three if it is a cold day. Cold days never seem to discourage the Large Dark Olives hatching—I have seen these flies spreading their wings gaily in snow-showers— but cold often delays the process a little.

During an early Spring, you may well discover Medium Olives— either *Baëtis vernus* or *Baëtis tenax*—hatching out as well, as April wears on. If you see flies on the water with high dusky-coloured wings, those will be Large Dark Olives. The best artificial fly, then, will be a good Rough Olive, or a Blue Upright or perhaps a Dark Olive. If the natural flies are a fraction smaller, and rather lighter in colour, they are nearly bound to be Medium Olives. A good Medium Olive or an Olive Dun will do quite well, but over and over again a Gold-Ribbed Hare's Ear has proved itself an even more killing fly when Medium Olives are about. And then there is Greenwell's Glory—an extremely useful fly which serves for either a Dark or Medium Olive.

The nymphs of both the Large Dark and Medium Olives like living in very well-oxygenated water. Shallow, fastish water is better oxygenated than slow, deep, smooth water. This means that the shallows of a chalk stream are better places to fish than the deeps during April. More fly will be hatching and wherever the fly hatches in strength trout will begin to feed.

One other possible fly in April is the Grannom. The Grannom, unlike the Olives, is a caddis-fly, or sedge-fly. All flies of this type, when they are not in the air, keep their wings folded back over their bodies. Grannoms also have a habit of struggling along over the top of the water, kicking up a bit of a commotion and leaving a wake behind them, instead of letting themselves be carried along smoothly by the current until they fly away.

The Grannom is one of the few sedge-flies which ever hatches *en masse*. It does not appear on all trout streams, but where it does the trout sometimes have a feast and fishing with an artificial Grannom can be very good.

Just occasionally there may be no hatch of fly at all. At these times your best hope lies in finding a trout feeding on nymphs. Even when they are not about to hatch, nymphs often seem to go through periods of activity which expose them to trout. These periods may occur when the nymphs themselves decide to feed or perhaps when they make mass migrations from one weed-bed to another.

If a trout is darting from side to side under the water, obviously feeding on something, he may take a sunk nymph. So it is well worthwhile dropping one over him. Even when the trout is not in view you often see surface signs of underwater disturbances—bow waves, boils, humps and barely-distinguishable swirls—all made by nymphing trout.

Nymph-fishing, however, is an art in itself and there will be more to say about it later on. Early-season fishing on the chalk streams has just one slight disadvantage. You cannot really have a day's fishing. All your sport will be crowded into a fairly brief period during the hatch. The Large Dark Olives may hatch for one or two hours and the Medium Olives for a little longer, so that if both these flies follow each other on the water you may have as much as three or four hours of good fishing. But you will seldom have more, because you will be unlikely to catch many trout before or after the fly is on the scene. The long-drawn-out hatches of mid-summer are still to come and there will be no evening rise till June. Another trouble is that even the trout you do catch may not yet be in perfect condition.

If I had my choice of rivers to visit in April, I should go to Scotland, or to the North Country, or the West Country, where the season starts earlier and the trout are fatter and keener. The March Brown will probably be over but the trout will have started to feed on the surface to other flies. They will be eager to take full advantage of floating food at almost any time of the day.

In the West Country, for instance, you can catch trout from after breakfast till sunset, and enjoy the open air and the country for as long as the sun is in the sky. The middle of the day will still provide the peak hours for the dry fly but there will be no time when you need consider yourself foolish to be fishing it. Besides, the wild daffodils and primroses and wood anemones during early spring in the West Country have to be seen to be believed. Not all your trout will be caught by chalk-stream methods. On the chalk streams you usually wait till you see a rise and then you settle down to catch the trout that made it. On West Country streams such as the Tamar you can certainly do this with the trout you spot rising but when there are no insects on the water you have to go and search for the trout with your fly.

That is the main difference between the two sorts of fishing, between the chalk streams and other streams. On the Test and Itchen and rivers like them food is so abundant that the trout do not have to feed all day. When food is readily available, during a hatch of fly for instance, the trout will feed well but afterwards they will sink to the bottom of the river to rest and digest, and nothing you can do will tempt them in the slightest. But trout in streams like the Tamar are not nearly so lucky. There is far less food. They cannot afford to let any edible morsel pass them by and so they are on the lookout practically all day long.

Sometimes there are splendid rises on these streams. But there is no cause for despair if not a single fish can be seen breaking the surface. Even in those circumstances, it is possible to catch plenty of trout by 'fishing the water'—that is, by casting a fly in promising places.

At the times when flies hatch, the trout will rise. You can go from fish to fish, casting over each one with a good chance of catching him. The trout rise a little faster than they do on the chalk streams, and you have to strike a little more quickly. Among the likely flies to hatch will be Olives, sedges, stone-flies and smuts.

The Olives are the same as the ones that hatch on the chalk streams. There may be a few sedges and stone-flies about as well (though it is a little early in the year for many species of sedge). If they hatch they can sometimes be seen not only on the water but also in the air and crawling about on the stones and bushes by the side of the river. They are easier to identify when they are at rest. Both sorts of fly carry their wings, not upright, but folded over their bodies. There is a difference, however. A sedge's wings are humped over its back like a sloping roof while a stone-fly's are folded much closer, usually flat and flush with the body or occasionally, as with Willow-flies and Needle-flies, like a thin sheath.

Many sedges wait till the evening to hatch—but the Grannom is an exception, and so is the Grey Flag. Both hatch during the daytime. There are three or four separate species of sedge-fly commonly called Grey Flag or Grey Sedge. They vary in size but are all coloured grey, and the trout feed on them at several stages. They feed on the ascending pupae and hatching flies during the day and again on the spent flies in the evening, when they fall on the water after laying their eggs. The Grey Flag is a river-dweller rather than a lake-dweller and a Silver Sedge serves as a reasonable imitation of it.

Stone-flies offer fewer chances to the trout. They crawl onto land to hatch, which means that the only time when they are of any use to a dry-fly fisherman is after they have laid their eggs and died on the water. The trout, however, do feed on them while they are crawling along the bottom on their hatching journey, and many North Country fishermen enjoy great sport fishing with the live larvae or 'creepers'. These they collect from under the stones in the river.

It is worth-while keeping a watch for the odd stone-fly falling on the stream during April. The trout will take them. A Partridge and Orange or Grey Duster will catch trout when the Early Brown Stone-fly is about, and a good imitation of the Large Stone-fly may catch them when this unmistakeable, outsize, rather fearsome-looking insect is on the wing. Then there may perhaps be trout rising to Reed-Smut as well. On warm days, particularly in smooth water with a little shade, you may see four or five dimpling the water every other second, all within a few square feet.

These trout will be smutters. Each individual fly is so small that they have to work very hard to get a square meal out of them. A Black Gnat is probably the best fly here but often when the trout are fairly innocent they will treat an imitation of something larger as manna from Heaven and swallow it accordingly. I always try smutters with whatever fly I happen to have on my cast first, and then change to a Black Gnat if they will not take it. If you open the stomach of one of these trout you will find that it contains a huge black mass of partially-digested smut.

You can see that there is quite a variety of fly on a West Country stream in April, but they do not hatch so regularly as on the chalk streams. Nor are the hatches so big. I have found on the Tamar, for instance, that I probably catch about half a daily bag of trout by casting to rising fish—perhaps more, perhaps less, according to the quantity of fly on the day—and the other half by casting a fly where trout may be lying, in fact by fishing the water.

Where *will* trout lie? To fish the river successfully a person has to be able to think like a trout. Where could you lie, if you were a hungry trout? Trout never like battling with the current if they can help it. They prefer to lie out of the direct force of the stream. But on the other hand it is the stream that brings them their food, so what are they to do? Like sensible creatures they compromise by finding some sheltered spot within reach and eyesight of a steady, not a raging current.

These sheltered spots can be provided by weeds, by rocks, by eddies and backwaters, and of course by dips in the riverbed. There is always shelter behind a rock. Also, perhaps less obviously, there is shelter in front of it. The current starts changing its course to by-pass or flow over a rock just before reaching it, leaving a cushioned space of water just upstream where trout often lie.

By watching the top of the water, you can learn how to 'read' the river like a book. Where two gentle currents converge, for instance, the food from both will be concentrated and a trout will probably be waiting. Where rough water changes to smooth, there will usually be a hollow in the riverbed. The stream will have dug out a lovely little resting-place for trout, from which they can dash to grab flies or anything else that comes down. If you put your fly over one of these hollows, however small it seems, you may well catch its tenant, or one of its tenants.

It is a sort of guessing-game, in fact, and you get better and better at it as time goes on. It is fun anyway. You work your way up the river, flicking your fly into all the places where you think a trout may be. Every now and then you will be right. A trout will nose up and your fly will go down and with luck the trout will soon be in the net. After a few days you make the pleasant discovery that you are getting far more rises and far more trout per hundred casts than you ever did when you started, because you are now beginning to think like the trout.

The trout will be less choosy and finicky than on the chalk streams, and exact imitation of the fly on the water will not be so important. This is not to say that exact imitation can be completely discounted. A good imitation of the fly hatching will usually catch more trout than any other pattern. Some trout, however, will take an imitation of almost any fly. The local tackle-shop, wherever you are, will supply you with the most effective local tyings. Pheasant Tails and Ginger Quills are great stand-bys in many places. If you fish in fairly fast water they need to be tied rather larger than for chalk-stream fishing, because they can then be seen better on the ripples. Another good fly for rough water is the Grey Wulff, because it is tied with animal hair and floats excellently. Any of these flies is a good one to fish until a definite hatch takes place of some fly which you can imitate.

Rain-fed streams, subject to flooding, normally cut a pretty deep channel for themselves. When the winter floods are over, and the water-level goes down, the banks may be several feet high. This means wading. If you do not wade, you are so far above your fish that they can see you easily and will probably be frightened. So you get into the water in your thigh-waders and move cautiously upstream from fish to fish or from likely lie to likely lie, casting a short line. Once you are in the water you can get remarkably close to the trout.

These trout may seem small compared with chalk-stream or reservoir trout. There is a danger of chalk-stream fishermen and reservoir fishermen getting snobbish about the size of their fish. On the Tamar, for instance, the limit is eight inches and it takes three or four trout to make up the pound. On Dartmoor the limit is lower, only six inches. On several Irish streams that I have fished no trout are put back and they are all served up for breakfast next morning looking like a plateful of sardines. But even the smallest trout can be great sport. The answer is not to expect monsters. What you lose in weight, you make up in enjoyment and quality. And you never know whether your next cast may not produce a prodigious trout for the river, perhaps a trout of a pound or more, which would be nothing to be ashamed of even on the chalk streams.

As a change from the dry fly there is always the wet fly. When the water is clear the dry fly may account for more fish but when it is a little cloudy the wet fly may be as good or even better. The trout caught on the dry fly are usually larger. A wet fly sometimes seems irresistible to fingerlings and salmon-parr, some of which hook themselves quite badly so that you have to spend agonizing moments easing out the barb while the poor little fish wriggle about. Also, with the dry fly, you have the pleasure of actually seeing the trout take the fly.

Some experts in the West Country fish dry and wet at the same time and this can be a very successful method. They use two flies on their cast, a wet fly as a tail-fly and a dry fly half way up as a dropper. They cast upstream and the trout can take their choice. If they prefer the dry fly, the fisherman sees them rise. If they choose the wet fly, the dry fly acts as a sort of float which bobs visibly so that the fisherman knows when to strike. Sadly enough, many West Country streams are now far less productive than they used to be, mainly because of agricultural pollution.

Heavy rain is often the greatest enemy of the holidaying trout fisherman on a rain-fed stream. When the skies open and a downpour starts, salmon fishermen may be pleased because every spate brings up fresh, bright salmon from the sea. But all it means to the trout fisherman is coloured water in which even a wet fly fails to attract trout. That is when the locals go out and catch fine 'messes' of trout on the worm. The fly-enthusiast can do nothing except sit and twiddle his thumbs (unless he can fish a nearby lake) until the water clears. The higher up a river he is the sooner will fishing become possible again. The little tributaries clear first, within a few hours, then the upper stretches of the main stream and finally the lower reaches, which may take two or three days.

Once May starts, chalk-stream fishing really comes into its own. One great asset of the chalk streams is that when you get up in the mornings you never have to scan the skies quite so anxiously. A strong downstream wind may make fishing tricky but rain will seldom make it impossible by clouding the water. This is because the chalk streams are spring-fed. And by May the water-meadows are beginning to look really pleasant again. They will be greener and lusher than before, and there will be yellow king-cups and white ladies' smocks in them. Although the evening rise has not yet begun, Olives, Iron Blues and Black Gnats will be on the water for long hours during each and every day and spinners may fall in the late afternoon.

The Large Dark Olives will be over, but there will be plenty of Medium Olive hatches and there may be some Pale Wateries. The Greenwell's Glory and Gold-Ribbed Hare's Ear will again be good flies for the Medium Olive. It is not entirely clear why trout find the latter so attractive, though a possible theory is that the tying of the body may suggest a fly hatching out of its nymphal shuck.

Pale Wateries will hatch from the first warm days of late Spring till the end of the season. There are four flies commonly called Pale Wateries. They are: the Pale Watery itself (*Baëtis bioculatus*); the Small Dark Olive (*Baëtus scambus*); the Large Spurwing (*Centroptilum pennulatum*); and the Small Spurwing (*Centroptilum luteolum*). All, to a greater or lesser degree, look fairly 'pale' on the water—even the Small Dark Olive. The trout do not seem as fond of them as they are of the other Olives and Iron Blues, but Pale Wateries will hatch on hot days when other flies will not. So they are a mainstay in warm weather. If the trout are taking small, light-coloured flies a Tups Indispensable or a Little Marryat should catch them.

There is also one important land-bred fly which falls on the water in May, though not in such numbers as in August, and that is the Black Gnat. May and late August are its favourite times, for it is never seen much in mid-summer. The Black Gnat—*Bibio johannis* and other species—is not an up-winged fly. When you notice tiny little dark bundles floating down the stream, with just a touch of white on their backs where they have folded their wings, these will be the Black Gnats that trout always seem to take so eagerly despite their small size. Usually, they take any good imitation of a Black Gnat just as eagerly.

But of all the flies that trout like perhaps the Iron Blue—*Baëtis pumilus*—is their favourite. The Iron Blue, again, is not a big fly. Its wings are blue-black, even darker than the wings of the Dark Olive, and its body is darker as well, so that from a distance it simply looks a small, jet-black, up-winged fly. When Iron Blues hatch out the trout usually decide to have a real feed and fishermen have a good day. Tackle-dealers sell both winged and hackled imitations of the Iron Blue. Tyings of the male fly often have a twist of red on the hook and I personally have a rather irrational feeling that this does attract more trout than the unrelieved darkness of the female fly.

Cold, windy, rainy May days lead to big hatches of Iron Blue, so that if the weather is hardly suitable for sunbathing the flies may provide plenty of compensation. Cold weather has another advantage, too. When nymphs hatch out into flies they stand on the water, supported by the surface-film, until their wings are firm and ready for flight. Then they take off. In warm weather this happens very quickly. But when there is no sun and the air has a bite to it, the flies stay on the water longer and the trout have a far greater chance to take them. More fish feed in consequence. All through the summer the fisherman has the best of both worlds. If the weather is fine he can enjoy it, but if it is not his fishing may be better.

Sedges are not very common on the chalk streams in May, though the Welshman's Button—a smallish dark-brown sedge—sometimes appears on the water. Then an imitation of it may catch fish.

On lakes and reservoirs, the up-winged flies you see will not be the same as those on rivers. The most common ones to hatch in the first part of the season will probably be the Sepia Dun and Claret Dun (*Leptophlebia marginata* and *Leptophlebia vespertina*). They are large dark flies, about the same size as a Large Dark Olive—but they each have three tails, whereas the Large Dark Olive has only two. They can be imitated by a Sepia or Claret Dun—or by a Red Quill.

As late Spring approaches, Pond Olives (*Cloëon dipterum*) will begin to appear and will hatch throughout the summer. These are also darkish in colour, but a little smaller, and on close examination you will see that they have no rear wings. They have only two wings instead of four—a rare feature for any up-winged fly. Either a Rough Olive or a Grey Duster will imitate them.

Throughout the late mornings and early afternoons in May fish should rise well. Warm, sunny days may bring out fly as early as half-past ten and a few fish may feed on nymphs preparing to hatch before the proper rise begins. On colder days neither fly nor trout may show themselves until one o'clock or two o'clock or even three o'clock. There is a record in my fishing diary of one day when I watched a lifeless river till five in the afternoon. Just as I was starting to go home in despair some Iron Blues began to hatch, then more and more. For two hours afterwards I had some of the best fishing of my life. I have never seen quite so late a hatch since that time but the memory of it has always helped me not to give up hope too early.

It is more common, however, to see falls of spinner than hatches of fresh fly in the late afternoon. Most spinners like dancing and laying their eggs best when there is not too much wind—but they do seem to prefer a slight, gentle breeze to a dead calm. In May, some spinners may lay their eggs and die in the morning and early afternoon but seldom in sufficient numbers to interest the trout. After tea there are usually more of them, often enough to make the trout take up their feeding-stations again. Spinners, unfortunately, are not at all obvious as they float down the stream on their last dying journey with their wings spread flat on the water. They are practically invisible except from directly above and the best sign of a trout taking spinner is his rise-form. When a trout takes an up-winged fly—a dun—he frequently sticks his nose up above the water. The rise is quite large. When he takes a spinner he does it far more gently, merely sipping it down from the top of the water. Occasionally he may skim if off the surface and show his back in a sort of roll but in neither case will a fisherman see very much of his nose.

So if trout seem to be rising quietly to invisible surface-food they are often taking spinner.

If you peer closely at the water beneath you, you can see the spinners floating down. They may be quite dead, in which case their wings will be outstretched, or they may have a little life left in them and still be holding their wings upright. Sometimes one wing becomes entangled in the surface-film, giving them a crumpled lop-sided appearance.

The different sorts of spinner can be told apart by their size and colour. This is not nearly so easy a business as recognizing duns because male and female spinners of the same species never look alike and both of them have changed considerably since the dun stage. However, the female spinners are really the only important

5. KNEELING while playing a fish can often shorten the playing time, especially when there is good cover on the bank to kneel behind. The less the trout sees of his captor, the more quickly and quietly he will come to the net. Admittedly this Itchen trout has thrown himself clear of the water – for there is little bank-cover in early April – but the principle is a good one. The fisherman is Jack Hemingway, son of Ernest Hemingway and one of the best-known conservationists-cum-fishermen in the USA.

6. THIS PHOTOGRAPH was taken at Chew Valley, where Colonel Philip Pardoe is about to net a good trout. His rod is held well up, as of course it should be, so that the tip can absorb and cushion the shock of any sudden rushes that the fish may make. Good opportunities for the dry fly may be less frequent on still waters than on most rivers, but when conditions are right it can nevertheless provide some very memorable and exciting fishing.

7. LOOSE LINE at a fisherman's feet is always a danger. When a trout makes a powerful run the line may well catch in twigs on the ground – or for that matter in the floor boards of a boat – and cause a break. When a fish runs directly towards the fisherman, it may indeed be necessary to pull in line by hand in order to keep contact. But any such line should be wound up – and the fish then played from the reel – as quickly as possible.

8. ONE MORTAL SIN is to leave long strands of nylon lying around anywhere in the countryside. Birds will walk into the nylon, find their legs inextricably entangled in it, and die. The photograph here shows how to deal with unwanted nylon. Roll it into a small coil and then cut it into short pieces. Treated like this it will cause no danger to wildlife.

5

6

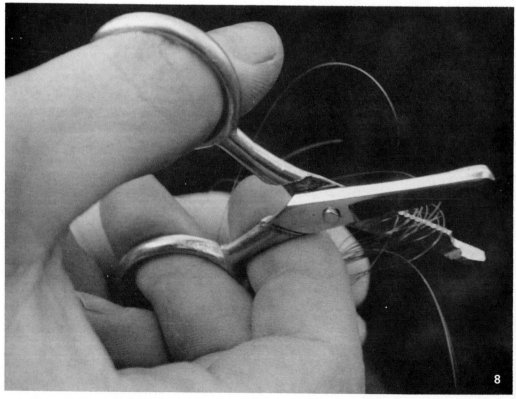

ones. Most of the males die on land and do not fall on the water. Another lucky thing is that a comparatively small selection of artificial spinners seems to serve quite well for a large variety of natural insects.

The female spinner of the Large Dark Olive—sometimes called a Large Red Spinner—is pretty big and has a dark red body. The wings are colourless except for a few dark visible veins. An artificial Red Spinner imitates it very well.

It is more difficult to distinguish the spinners of other Olives, also those of Pale Wateries and some lake flies. Many of them have colourless wings and brown bodies ranging from dark brown to amber. Their exact colours vary a little from water to water and also according to climatic conditions. But if the spinners on the water— whether it be still water or running water—are fairly dark, a Lunn's Particular will imitate them well. And if they are light, a Little Amber Spinner or a Lunn's Yellow Boy will catch fish. A Pheasant Tail is another very good fly when Olive spinners are falling—and this includes the spinners of Pond Olives. (Many artificial spinners are tied with their wings stretched out so that they lie flat on the water and look like dead flies.) Fish often take artificial spinners more readily than to they do the artificial duns, because a dead fly cannot flutter. A freshly hatched fly often does flutter, which is something that no artificial fly yet tied can imitate.

There is one spinner still left to describe, often the most successful of all. Trout love the spinners of the Iron Blue as much as the duns. The female Iron Blue spinner is a tiny fly with white colourless wings and a dark mahogany-red body. It looks just like an artificial fly called a Houghton Ruby and the Houghton Ruby is by far the best imitation of it. When these spinners are on the water you should catch plenty of fish.

You will find middle-May to be one of the best times on the chalk streams. The trout rise freely. And the water-meadows become love- lier still as the month wears on. Now even the ashes—those late comers to the summer scene—will be busy covering themselves with leaves. Before long the hawthorn will begin to blossom and the ranunculus will push its white flowers up above the surface of the water.

But before then something else will appear on the surface, a large yellow insect, the lone vanguard of armies to follow. You will probably see a Mayfly.

CHAPTER 8

Mayfly Interlude

The Mayfly sometimes sends fish into frenzies of greed. But it can also send fishermen into frenzies of frustration. The only thing that can be predicted with any certainty at all about Mayflies is the approximate time of their arrival on the water. Whether Spring is late or early may make some difference. Even so, the Mayflies usually begin to appear on the water roughly when they are expected, within a few days.

However this time does vary from place to place. On the Lambourn in Berkshire, for instance, the Mayflies begin hatching well at the end of May. But on the Kennet—the river of which the Lambourn is actually a tributary—they seldom hatch until early June. The Mayfly season on the Test and Avon starts between May 18th and May 23rd. On some great Irish Mayfly loughs, where huge trout are caught by dapping with live Mayflies, the big hatches start in mid-May, but on others they start weeks later.

A fortnight or even more before the proper hatches begin, a few single insects will appear every day, and there will be little flurries of them in the second week of the fortnight. Fishermen will begin to roam optimistically up and down the river-bank, hoping for an early hatch. But if they try to fish with a Mayfly then, they seldom have much luck because the trout are not nearly so impatient. They will often feed on tiny Black Gnats in preference to the few succulent-looking Mayflies about. Even when the Mayflies do arrive in force the trout sometimes ignore them for a day or two. The first big hatches seem to frighten trout rather than attract them. They tend to treat the outsize insects rather warily, to leave them alone till they find out a bit more about them, and if possible to let the next-door fish do a little tasting before they feed themselves.

The small fish usually start rising to Mayflies first. Suddenly there will be an excited splash, and perhaps a second one, as an undersized trout comes half out of the water to grab a fluttering fly. Trout often rise to Mayflies with a splash, though the larger fish and the steadier feeders may take more quietly. These will be the trout worth catching.

And a truly thrilling sight it is when they come on the feed. Monsters, whose presence you may never even have suspected in the river, leave their hides and begin gulping down Mayfly after Mayfly. This is the real signal for a dry-fly fisherman. When big trout start feeding steadily, you know that it is time for a Mayfly to replace the Hare's Ear or Black Gnat on your cast. The Mayfly carnival is open at last.

Most fisherman find a sort of magic in Mayflies year after year. Here the life-history of many river-insects can be seen on a really grand scale. You can watch the stick-like nymphs come up to the surface and float there motionless for a few seconds until a split quickly appears down their backs. Through the split emerges a crumpled lump which then expands suddenly as if a mastless little boat had grown a sail in a few scant seconds. The whole insect struggles out of its prison, stands for a while on the water and then takes off clumsily, leaving the dead, useless, discarded nymphal shuck behind it. It flies badly at first. Perhaps it makes several landings on the water before it reaches the bank. Perhaps it never reaches the bank—since trout, swallows, swifts and so on take a heavy toll of hatching Mayflies. Watching these Mayflies hatch is rather like watching a fairy-tale unfold itself. It is a story of transformation and re-birth. The ugly, burrowing nymphs, who have spent at least two years embedded in silt and mud, suddenly gain the freedom of the air and are all changed into Prince Charmings and Beautiful Princesses. Every Beast becomes a Beauty. But they are only a short space away from the end of their lives. As nymphs they can feed but they cannot mate, and as flies they can mate but they have no mouths. They cannot feed. So your hatching Mayfly has made its choice between love and life.

These Mayflies provide many red-letter days. But a bad day is the most humiliating experience possible. This is what happens. You arrive at the water after breakfast to discover several trout lying near the surface apparently waiting for Mayflies. But no Mayflies are hatching, so you decide to wait too. Nothing occurs till about three o'clock, when a few flies begin to hatch. The trout pay no attention to them at all. They do not seem interested. Apart from the fact that they have taken up feeding positions they might as well be asleep. You try casting over them but fail to bring them up. Then, about five o'clock, some more Mayflies float down the stream and all the trout immediately seem to go mad.

Before long there are fish splashing around on every side. The whole water is a scene of frantic activity with hundreds of Mayflies skimming over the surface and birds practically colliding with trout in their haste to pick them up. But somehow you cannot find a steadily feeding fish. As soon as you mark a trout he unaccountably stops rising. Nevertheless there are so many trout in evidence that you think you are bound to come across a regular feeder at some stage. And perhaps you do. You cast over him. He takes Mayflies to the right of you, Mayflies to the left of you, Mayflies all round you, but never your own fly.

Eventually you manage to deceive one innocent fish. He rises. You strike and miss him. The same thing happens again later, and yet again. Finally you begin to cast in a sort of panic, wondering why on this day of all days, when you should be reaping the Mayfly harvest, you cannot catch a single trout. Perhaps you never do, unless you foul-hook one who rolls playfully onto your fly in the course of his frolics.

There may be several reasons why a Mayfly day sometimes turns out badly. First of all a Mayfly is a very large mouthful for any trout. Many of them seem to like taking two or three Mayflies one after the other, then waiting a little before coming back for a second helping. So the trout rise spasmodically. Then again a Mayfly, because of its size, is probably more difficult than other flies to imitate success-fully. The shortcomings of the artificial may be very obvious. Often it is the struggling of the natural fly that fascinates trout. Occasionally they will let flies go by that make no movement, leaping to seize only those that flutter, and unfortunately nothing could look less like a lively Mayfly than the sodden bunch of feathers that you sometimes find on the end of your leader.

Again, trout frequently fail to get a Mayfly into their mouths, particularly when they rush at it excitedly. You often see them missing real Mayflies. At other times they seem to flop onto the natural flies without actually taking them, almost as if they were trying to drown them. So it is only to be expected that far fewer trout who rise to a Mayfly should be hooked than of those who rise to a smaller fly.

Of course none of these misfortunes occurs on a red-letter day. The trout rise consistently and steadily and it takes a great deal to frighten them. If you cast a Mayfly anywhere near them they grab it firmly. There is a great temptation to treat red-letter days as opportunities for slaughter. This is so wrong. They should really be days of big-game hunting, and the little fish who are so anxious to give themselves up can be left undisturbed to provide sport when the Mayfly season is over and done with.

The times of day at which Mayflies hatch are sometimes rather irregular. They usually hatch in the afternoons, probably about 3 p.m., but occasionally you see them in the mornings too. There may be several hatches during the day or only one. Quite often the flies even hatch at different times on different stretches of the same river, so that while one fisherman is having good sport his next-door neighbour—a mere hundred yards or so away—may not be able to find a solitary rising fish. On a very, very good Mayfly day there may even be enough fly on the water from mid-morning till dusk to keep trout continually interested, with never a dull moment for any fisherman.

There are a bewildering number of Mayfly tyings in the tackle-shops. Some are hackled, others are winged and they range in colour from pale yellow to the darkness of the Black Admiral. It seems amazing that so many different patterns should be supposed to imitate only two natural flies—for there are two normal species of Mayfly, very similar to each other indeed—but nevertheless they all seem to catch fish on good days. On bad days perhaps none of them will. Local advice is usually the best to take on which pattern to use. It is probably worth buying several different sizes as well, because if one size is consistently refused a smaller or larger one may easily work better.

Mayfly nymphs live in silt or gravel and they will thrive equally well in still or running water. This is because they create their own oxygen-flow. They burrow into the silt at the bottom of lakes and rivers and keep water flowing through their little tunnels by fanning their bodies with their gills. In fact, on many slow, deep pieces of water, where silt has been deposited, the Mayfly season is the only time of the year when dry-fly fishing is any good at all. Conditions there are probably not suitable for smaller flies, except for midges and some sedges, but when the Mayflies hatch the big trout do come up to the surface.

Some lakes, particularly in Ireland, have tremendous hatches of Mayfly. You can fish these lakes—usually from a boat—in the normal dry-fly way by casting your fly in the path of one of the huge trout you see cruising around. Or you can fish by dapping. In order to dap, you need a long rod of fourteen feet at least, a light blow-line, a hook, a live Mayfly and a breeze. The live Mayfly is impaled on the hook. You then let the breeze blow it out on the blow-line until you can touch it down on the surface of the lake. No part of the line or leader should lie on the water. You watch your Mayfly dancing on the wave. Then a seven-pound trout takes it under. You curb yourself, for when you dap you must not strike quickly. So you close your eyes, recite a long prayer in Gaelic, and tighten. Afterwards, if you are lucky, you may find yourself with what appears to be a bucking horse at the end of your line.

After the Mayflies have been hatching on the river for about a week the great evening dances of Mayfly spinners begin. The flies, having shed a coat, come out from the trees and bushes to dance and mate. A big Mayfly dance is an awe-inspiring sight. The spectacle may start at any time from four o'clock onwards. A little cloud of male spinners comes onto the stage, looking now like graceful aerial acrobats, instead of the clumsy fliers they were when they first hatched. They dance over the water, or over the meadows by the side of the stream, soaring up and down in their thousands.

Round the males the females dance singly. Every now and then a male will leave the corps-de-ballet, flying towards the female he has chosen and attach himself to her. For a while they fly locked together in the air and then they sink down into the grass. Very shortly afterwards the female takes wing again to lay her eggs on the water, where she eventually falls exhausted. She becomes a spent fly. In the meantime that male flies off as well and may even rejoin the dancers but only for the few moments left to him before he also dies.

Most of the males die on land but nearly all the females die on the water. They fly close to the surface, dipping down now and again so that they just brush the stream and a cluster of eggs is washed off their bodies, a few at a time. The eggs sink slowly to the bottom where they will hatch into nymphs in future days. As the afternoon wears into evening, more and more Mayflies come to join the dance. Soon the air is full of them. I have known evenings when you could not see more than a few yards for Mayflies, when they alighted in hundreds on your coat, on your trousers, all over your body, and when all you could hear was the thin, brittle clatter of thousands of small wings. The sheer quantity of them can be stupefying.

Nature appears to be in a wasteful mood. Here are countless millions of female Mayflies all in the process of egg-laying. They will lay wherever they can find room or wherever there is water. They will lay in ditches and puddles, and if it has been raining they will lay on the wet, gleaming surfaces of roads. All these eggs will die quickly since they need oxygen even before they hatch into nymphs.

Female Mayflies lay about six thousand eggs apiece. Even if these are laid where they have some small chance of living, as they normally are, very few ever reach maturity. Some become covered with mud and literally choke. Most of them are eaten by insects or small animals before they hatch out into flies.

It is a somewhat sad sight to see all the dead, spent Mayflies floating downstream after egg-laying. Expressions like 'You could walk across the river on them' seem very nearly credible when you look at these Mayflies drifting down in dense masses, wing-tip to wing-tip, with scarcely a glimmer of water between them. Fishing is useless, since what hope has your fly among so many? At the end of the evening the dancing flies have disappeared but the banks of the river are littered and piled high with corpses. Weed beds are covered with them, weed-racks are blocked by them, until by dusk the whole stream is one vast open graveyard for Mayflies.

Luckily, these tremendous Mayfly dances do not happen every evening nor does every river support such large quantities of fly. If they did, fishing with the spent Mayfly would not provide such good sport as it nearly always does. Usually when the Mayfly season is a week or so old, and the Mayfly spinners begin to dance, your chances of catching trout are practically doubled. You can catch them every day while the fresh flies hatch and again while the spent flies fall. A perfect evening should bring out enough spinners to keep the fish feeding on them well but not so many that you have to stand with a useless rod in your hand and watch the trout taking one fly in every hundred.

For some reason the imitation of the Mayfly spinner is called a Spent Gnat. It is certainly spent, but it is certainly not a Gnat. Often you find fresh Mayflies and spent Mayflies coming down the river at the same time, and then the trout may be feeding on both—or on only one of them. In the latter case it pays to watch carefully and find out which.

Mayfly spinners are easy to distinguish from fresh flies when they are finally dead and floating with their wings flat. But sometimes when they are still dying and have their wings upright, they look rather like the fresh flies. That is, in shape. Their colours are quite different. In the air, with the light shining through it, a Mayfly spinner looks beautiful, but on the water it looks almost dirty. The wings have dark veins in them and the body is grey, becoming brown near the tail. Even from a distance it can be told by the fact that it appears much darker in colour than a freshly-hatched dun.

Not nearly so many fish are pricked or missed during a fall of spent Mayflies as they are during a hatch of fresh duns. The flies are not fluttering at this stage, so a trout tends to take each fly more deliberately and steadily. You seldom see trout missing the natural spinners, while they often miss the fresh flies. If too many spinners fall on the main stream for good fishing, the side-streams and carriers may be better. There are usually less Mayflies in these little streams so that the trout in them are more ready to take every single fly that comes down.

Mayflies hatch properly for a fortnight or a little longer. When are they at their best? Major Waller Hills, in his book 'Summer on the Test', put forward the theory that the fourth and twelfth days were the most likely for a big basket. So far as any theory in fishing can prove itself correct, this theory does. He explained that on the fourth day the trout had become accustomed to the Mayflies and were no longer wary of them, but on the other hand they were not yet gorged. And by the twelfth day they began to sense that the hatches were falling off and were determined to make the most of them while they lasted.

Even in the middle of the Mayfly season it is a great mistake to ignore the smaller flies. They can be very useful on many days. Before the Mayflies start hatching in the morning, the trout often rise to a small fly far better than to a Mayfly. And I can remember one evening when Mayfly spinners were falling and the trout were rising furiously and I could catch none of them on a Spent Gnat. I eventually discovered they were not feeding on Mayflies at all, and when I changed rather belatedly to a Lunn's Particular I immediately began catching fish.

The Mayfly is not an unmixed blessing to fishermen. Wherever Mayflies hatch, and wherever the trout feed well on them, there may for a little while be an aftermath when the gorged trout seem contemptuous of smaller flies. But this does not always happen. And on stocked rivers it is usually the custom, once the Mayfly is over, to put in a number of new fish who have never even seen it. Some fishermen, however, prefer stretches of water where there are no Mayflies at all, because sport throughout the summer is sometimes less of a boom-and-slump affair. But even so, who would be so foolish as to refuse an invitation to fish the Mayfly in its season?

CHAPTER 9

Nymph-Fishing and the Evening Rise

Nymph-fishing consists of catching a trout on an imitation of a fly before it has hatched. The imitation has to be where trout are feeding on the natural, which is often well below the surface. So nymph-fishing is perhaps not dry-fly fishing in the truest and strictest sense of the term. In a way it is more akin to wet-fly fishing, because whenever a trout takes a sunken wet fly (as opposed to a large and brightly-coloured 'lure') he usually does so under the impression that it is some underwater creature, probably a nymph. In fact, dry-fly purists used to denounce nymph-fishing roundly, as being an unfair way of catching well-bred chalk-stream trout. Some of them also carried on a long argument with the man who first recognised and wrote about all the enjoyment and success to be had out of this form of fishing—Mr. G. E. M. Skues. But Skues stuck firmly to his viewpoint. He said that an artificial nymph was a fair imitation of a natural insect, exactly as a dry fly was.

And of course he was right. By now the nymph is established as a skilful and perfectly legitimate way of catching trout on most stretches of the chalk streams, and nearly everywhere else besides. But since nymph-fishing is still frowned upon on a few dry-fly-only waters, it is always wise to find out the local rules about it before fishing anywhere.

A nymph will certainly not catch trout at all times. It is a specific medicine, on the chalk streams anyway, for those trout who are actually taking natural nymphs. It does give a fisherman a chance to fish with some hope of success for these trout, when they refuse duns. Before a rise starts trout may spend a little time feeding on nymphs. And if the hatch is very sparse they may find better feeding below the surface than on the surface. And some trout seem to prefer nymphs to duns even when there is a good hatch. When you examine the stomach-contents of trout it is amazing how many nymphs you nearly always discover in them, which shows that trout may often treat nymphs as their bread-and-butter and duns merely as jam.

This is not really surprising, because although trout have no control over hatches of fly at all, they can always go and hunt for nymphs in the weed beds when they feel hungry. In waters where plenty of duns hatch, and at the times of the year when they hatch frequently, trout will usually come to the surface to feed. But in waters of a different sort, or during weather when duns will not hatch, nymphs may become their staple diet. Many of these nymphs will be eaten by trout who are grubbing around deep in the weed-beds, or among the stones at the bottom of the stream, and are therefore seldom visible, even less get-at-able. Many other nymphs, however, will be swallowed more or less in the open by trout waiting for them to be brought down by the current.

When the nymphs are just about to hatch, or actually in the process of doing so, trout can often make a good meal of them. Then the nymphs come up to the surface of the water, break their way through the surface-film and float there for a short time while they hatch. Just a word here about surface-film. Water in contact with air always tends to cling together on its outer surface. It forms a film, which is why needles can be floated on water. There is always a surface-film on the top of a lake or river. In a way this is a help to insects, because they can stand on it, walk on it and generally treat it as humans might treat ice-covered water. It will support any small water-resistant object, such as a dry fly. But nymphs sometimes have difficulty in breaking through it and duns may become entangled in it, so that they cannot fly away. Scum on the surface often traps flies before they succeed in taking off.

While nymphs are on or near the surface-film and in the process of hatching, trout find them easy to catch. The nymphs are without cover and in full view of the fish and, although they may struggle a little, they do not flutter like a dun nor dart sharply through the water as swimming nymphs do at other times. So the trout take them quietly, without fuss of excitement.

If the nymphs are floating on the surface-film, a trout's rise may be rather like a spinner-rise. But often the trout takes the nymphs before they get there, and then his rise makes only a small hump on the surface, if that. The best imitation of a hatching nymph is the floating type called an 'emerger'.

Trout also feed on nymphs which are not necessarily going to hatch straight away, but which have temporarily left cover. The nymphs may be making a migration from one weed-bed to another. Or, if weeds have been cut, they may be escaping from drifting strands of it to a safer home. Or again, when they themselves are feeding, they may become rash and get swept away from their own weed-beds by the current. The trout are never slow to seize their opportunity to intercept the nymphs. These nymphs, however, are not all immobile. Some species make quick, spasmodic dashes through the water, so that the trout have to chase around and pursue them.

So trout, here, are frequently very active. They may move quite a long way from their original place to snap up the swimming nymphs. In shallow water they may give away their presence by plunging and flouncing about, leaving boils and bow-waves behind them. In deeper water, where they make no disturbance on the surface, they are usually more difficult to detect. The best hope, then, is to catch sight of the nymphing trout himself, which can often be done in clear, or fairly clear, water. The trout will probably be moving quickly and purposefully from side to side, opening and shutting his mouth from time to time as he takes a nymph.

Any of these nymphing trout may conceivably take a dun. But again they may not. If they are concentrating solely on the nymphs, it may be a waste of time to throw floating flies over them. Many a nymphing trout has been bombarded for hours with dry flies, to the complete disappointment of the fisherman concerned, who usually says afterwards: 'He *seemed* to be feeding well, but I just couldn't interest him'. That is why it is so helpful to be able to tell when a trout is taking nymphs, not duns. Even if you are fishing on water where the nymph is not allowed, you will at least know that here is a fish over whom you should not break your heart, and upon whom you should not spend all day, since he is unlikely to pay any attention to you.

Where the nymph is allowed in these circumstances, it must of course sink. The selection of an artificial should by rights pose a problem—since you will have no idea which species of nymph the trout appears to be so keen on—but in practice you will find that good all-round patterns usually work well. The Pheasant Tail and Grey Goose nymphs devised by Frank Sawyer are highly successful on most streams.

The sinking of the nymph can be greatly helped by the way in which it is tied. A nymph should be dressed very lightly, for otherwise it will offer too much resistance to the surface-film and will never slip through easily. The best sinking nymphs are now always 'weighted'—usually by winding fine wire round the body—to make them sink more readily.

If your nymph is not sufficiently 'weighted' it may sit stubbornly on the surface-film without sinking. Then a little fish-slime (or saliva) will help it to go under. By the time it reaches the trout it should be down to the level at which he is feeding—this needs nice judgement. The farther upstream you cast, the deeper it will sink before it reaches the trout. In a fast current, too, you must cast farther up than in a slow current. To stop the nymph sinking too deep, it is a good idea to grease the whole of your leader except for the last few inches.

A dragging nymph frightens trout far less frequently than a dragging fly on the surface, partly because it makes no wake—and partly because many natural nymphs make little darts and dashes through the water. In fact, the best way to interest a nymph-feeding fish is to give the artificial a little twitch just as it reaches him. He will often have it. This technique has come to be called the 'induced take' and it accounts for many trout.

When a trout accepts a well sunk nymph, the fisherman has to strike as he would with an ordinary dry fly. This is perhaps the most skilful and fascinating part of nymph-fishing. The skill lies in knowing exactly when to strike, and the fascination in finding an extremely firmly-hooked trout on the end of the line afterwards. Of course there is no difficulty about it, or very little, when the trout makes a well-defined hump or boil on the surface, but sometimes he takes the nymph very quietly beneath the surface, giving no clear indication of a rise. You have to watch the water like a hawk for the various signs which may mean the trout has the nymph in his mouth.

The most useful—and most reliable—of these signs is the motion of the nylon where it goes into the water a few inches from the nymph. If you watch it carefully, you can see it travelling down-stream at the pace of the current, until a trout takes the nymph, when it stops dead and then twitches or draws through the water as the trout moves down or away. The best time to strike is when the leader first stops, rather than when it draws, because in the first case the trout has seized the nymph in his mouth, while in the second case he is making off with it and may open his mouth at any time to get rid of it. For a fisherman with reasonably good eyesight, the checking of the leader is an invaluable message to say that a trout has found the nymph acceptable. Sometimes, admittedly, the nymph turns out to be caught up in some weed, but a few false alarms are far better than failing to strike when a trout does take the nymph.

Another message is the flash of a trout's flank or belly as he turns. Occasionally, as you gaze at the water where you think your nymph may be, you spy just the faintest glimmer of yellow and raise your hand to discover that you have hooked a trout. Skues called this the 'wink under water'.

If the trout is in full view, the fisherman may see him swim towards the nymph—or towards the place where the fisherman thinks the nymph is—open and shut his jaws and then turn to go back to his original position. Sometimes you cannot see the movement of his jaws, but the time to strike is at the precise moment of the trout's turning, not before. Then he is most likely to have his mouth shut, with the nymph inside it. The temptation to strike too early is very great. Whenever a trout can be seen coming towards a fly, an anxious person is only too liable to jerk up the rod-tip while the fish is still several feet away. A trout often follows a nymph for some way before seizing it, and it is all too easy to strike while the nymph is still only being inspected. As soon as he has taken it, he usually turns. So a wave coming along the surface of the water in the general direction of a fisherman's nymph is never a good signal to raise the rod. The trout is probably still approaching the nymph. When the wave starts to swirl and change direction, then is the time to strike.

Nymph-fishing is a very satisfying affair—when you see the sudden stopping of the leader, tighten at this slenderest of hints and then feel the rod bend in response. The sequence requires even more vigilance, if perhaps a little less delicacy, than to hook a fish taking duns. An advantage of nymph-fishing is that it gives you a second string to your bow. A fisherman with a nymph in his fly-box need never sit around in despair when there are no flies hatching. Even though no trout are rising at the surface, one or two may always be feeding on nymphs, and can sometimes be caught.

The nymph can be deadly on reservoirs as well as rivers. Patterns here tend to be a little more varied, and so are the different ways of fishing them. For instance, there are some patterns imitating small midge-pupae and these should be fished in or only just below the surface-film, which means greasing the leader right up to the end. Other patterns can be fished deeper. When you fish a nymph in still water you cast it out and then 'retrieve' it by drawing in line with your left hand. On occasions a fairly fast retrieve will catch trout. But often the best retrieve is a very slow and patient one—a little twitch every ten seconds or so. Brightly-coloured lures which imitate small fish are on the whole most attractive when they move quickly. But natural insects do not break speed records and artificial nymphs should seldom be hurried through the water.

Now for the evening rise. Once summer has started, this is another saver of many blank days. In flaming hot weather, when few flies have appeared on the water all morning and all afternoon, fishermen usually look forward eagerly to the evening, because the evening rise may be especially good. The hotter the day, the better the evening rise. Your sport may be fast and furious. You may catch several fish in a remarkably short time. You may land one of the huge fish who never condescend to rise during the daytime. You may do wonders. Or—you may find yourself getting more and more frustrated as the light fades and your time runs out. You can easily cast over dozens of rising trout for a frantic and quite fruitless half-hour, and go home disappointed at the end of it.

Trout sometimes seem to behave very illogically during the evening rise, as they may do during a hatch of Mayfly. But the evening rise seldom lacks for excitement, and whether you catch trout or not, it is always cheering to see them show themselves just before dusk. The evening rise is probably the most regular meal-time that the trout have. Even on apparently perfect fishing days, there may be no mass hatch of fly in the daytime, but there will usually be a rise of some sort in the evening from mid-June onwards.

On reservoirs the dry fly often comes into its own in the evening. During the day you may see few rises, and the few that you do see may be out of reach, but in the evening the trout often cruise close to the shore, showing themselves as they take surface-food. Even though lures, wet flies and nymphs may have been all that would catch them previously, a dry imitation of a midge or a sedge—or perhaps of a tiny *Caenis*—can do much damage at dusk.

On a river the overture to the evening rise normally starts about an hour before the sun dips below the horizon. Very few up-winged duns will be on the water then, but a good number of spinners should fall as long as the wind is not too strong. Some of the spinners may belong to the ordinary daytime species of fly. The most frequent spinner to visit the water on a summer evening, however, is the spinner of the Blue-winged Olive—*Ephemerella ignita*.

This fly—a highly important evening fly—is common in rivers and streams all over the country. It occasionally breeds in big lakes too. The female spinner is a palish brown and this has led to its rather apt name of Sherry Spinner. On the right sort of evening you can see thousands of these Sherry Spinners winging their way upstream in long columns to lay their eggs.

They make a very pretty sight against the light, and a very reassuring one, because they will soon fall spent on the water and the trout will rise to them. The artificial Sherry Spinner is an extremely effective fly when trout are feeding on the naturals, so much so that a fisherman often catches more during this time than during the evening rise proper. Sometimes the trout ignore the duns when they do eventually hatch, and go on taking spinners for as long as they fall. They may not always be Sherry Spinners, however, on some stretches of water a Lunn's Particular does even better.

Just as the sun begins to vanish, or perhaps just after its upper rim has disappeared, duns often start hatching. On the chalk streams, they will probably be Blue-winged Olives, flies with three tails, olive-coloured bodies and distinctively high, blue-grey wings. Less frequently they may be Yellow Evening Duns (*Ephemerella notata*), or Pale Evening Duns (*Procoleon pseudorufulum*)—the former of which is a yellow three-tailed fly, while the latter is a medium-sized fly with two tails and no hind-wings. Unless, and this is unlikely, the river is slow-flowing enough to harbour Pond Olives, the Pale Evening Dun is the only fly you are likely to find with only two wings.

Imitation can be tricky. There is no sure fly for the evening. When the Blue-winged Olive is hatching, most fishermen use an Orange Quill—largely because that grand old man Skues advised it. Although it may be heresy to say so, I have seldom found it very much use. Yes, it will occasionally catch a trout or two but for my money I prefer a Beacon Beige or a Kite's Imperial. There are artificial Yellow Evening Duns and Pale Evening Duns to match Yellow Duns and Pale Evening Duns. You can also use a Little Marryat to imitate the latter.

If there is a good hatch, many more trout usually feed than are ever seen during the day. But this is where the silly cussedness of the evening rise comes in. Often the river seethes with trout. In every square yard, you see a fish rising well. It seems impossible that they should not take an artificial fly and come to the net, one after another. Yet you cast to fish after fish, fighting a hurried and losing battle against the fast-approaching darkness, without being able to make one of them so much as notice your fly, let alone take it. There may be too many fly, or too great a variety of fly. Or the trout, perhaps more often than we think, may be feeding on midge-pupae. An artificial midge-pupa is an excellent last resort.

But this does not always happen. Trout may give themselves up readily while the flies hatch. A hatch of Blue-winged Olives seldom lasts longer than half-an-hour, and it may only last ten minutes. Then there will be no Ephemeropterans left on the water. But the fishermen could be found and all he could hear was the 'slamming of excitement to come. After a short lull, or even without any lull at all, he is very likely to hear a heavy-sounding splashy rise somewhere in the stream—which will mean that there are some sedge-flies about. It is usually worth waiting ten minutes or so to see if the trout begin to feed on sedges. One chalk-stream keeper I know always used to complain to me that whenever a sedge-rise started none of his fishermen could be found and all he could hear was the slamming of car-doors all around'.

Sedge-flies stay on the water later than Ephemeropterans. When the bats begin to appear, that is the time when trout, including big trout, may come up for sedges. Some of these large old trout may hide themselves for most of the day, only leaving their holts under the cover of darkness. The greater part of their food will probably be made up of young trout, minnows, crayfish and other fair-sized items, but they are often prepared to take a sedge. Very large trout are often caught at sedge-time.

So it is a good idea to tie a sedge onto the cast, holding the eye of the fly up to the light, before it gets too dark to do it at all. Most ordinary sedge-patterns are quite effective, a Cinnamon Sedge being one of the most popular. When trout take spent sedges, they do so very quietly. But when the sedges are hatching or laying their eggs, the trout splash and slash at them, because they scutter across the top of the water. At these times it often pays to drag the imitation deliberately. Trout who ignore the fly when it floats normally sometimes wallop up to it viciously when they see its wake.

There is one other rule which the sedge-fly allows you to break. On the chalk streams people usually fish for rising trout, and seldom cast a random fly, but a sedge at dusk is a permissible exception. It is often worth searching the river, or parts of the river, with a sedge when trout are not rising. But you have to know where the good trout are. Once you know the right spots, where the fish feed at dusk, you can frequently bring up some unexpectedly large fish. There is one particular stretch of the Itchen, just below a mill in the town of Winchester itself, which has very few Ephemeropterans in it. You seldom see a trout rising there. However, if you fish a sedge on this water in the late evening, you may well catch a trout of over two pounds.

While speaking of large fish, I really cannot resist telling the tale of the largest wild trout I ever met in Britain. He lived in a culvert, through which flowed a tiny stream, the merest ditch, only three yards wide and a couple of feet deep. It formed one of the headwaters of the Itchen. Up above the culvert were some watercress beds and a good many shrimps from them were washed downstream to provide rich feeding for trout where the flow concentrated in the culvert itself. I came upon this place when it was almost dark, and immediately below the culvert I could just make out a long dark shape lying on the pale gravel.

As I watched, the shape tilted up to take something by the side of the brick wall. My first cast was not a brilliant one, but luckily my sedge chanced to touch the brickwork and dropped off right onto the trout's head. The shape tilted again. I struck, and the next moment my reel was giving out line as the trout ran up the culvert. There he stayed doggedly. He wouldn't budge an inch, and there was little enough I could do to bring him back. Only an occasional throb on the line reassured me that I was not snagged. After about three minutes of this, he came back towards me. Then he swam round for some time in stately circles—and I saw him once or twice. I thought he was a very good fish—at least three pounds. My main worry was that a large tuft of floating weed had somehow become attached to the 3X leader.

After about ten minutes in all, the fish was ready for the net, and I realized for the first time just how big he was. The only way I could possibly accommodate him was to draw the net over his tail, and on up his body, till only his nose was outside. The frame of the net broke as I lifted him up the bank, but the mesh held and soon I had carried him safely at least twenty yards into the field. I killed him quickly but then had to wait another five minutes before my hands stopped shaking enough to remove the hook. The fish weighed well over seven pounds and I have never since caught such a large wild trout in this country. One advantage of catching a big trout like this is that it satisfies the more ambitious side of your nature. You are happier with small fish ever after. You no longer have to hope desperately, every time you go out fishing, that the trout of a lifetime will be around the next corner. You have already caught him. Whether you fish for six-inch trout in Scotland, or eight-inch trout in Devon, or two-pound rainbows in a reservoir, it makes no difference at all so long as the fishing is interesting. It is a great thing to catch one large trout.

CHAPTER 10

A Summer's Day

People who want to fish while they are on holiday seldom go in the middle of the summer except for family reasons. The early season is a better time for a fishing holiday. So is September—but you often hear July and August referred to as the 'dead months'. How true is this?

Where the Mayfly has come and gone again, fishing does tend to deteriorate immediately afterwards. But where there has been no Mayfly, good fishing may go on as long as the big, concentrated hatches of small fly last, probably until the end of June. For instance the first weeks in June are the best weeks of the whole year on the Upper Itchen, with magnificent hatches of Olives and Iron Blues. June is also very good on many rocky streams where the water is cold and the river-bed is unsuitable for Mayflies.

As the month draws to its close, however, the daytime hatches of fly begin to fall off. The flies will go on hatching throughout the summer, but with nothing like the same regularity, and seldom in the same numbers. The water-temperature rises. Streams, lakes and reservoirs are lower in depth, lower in oxygen. You will not often see a mass display of trout till the evening.

But daytime fishing in high summer is far from hopeless and it can be very enjoyable. There is scarcely ever a time when it is quite impossible to catch a good trout. The countryside looks lovely during July and August and the banks of well-fished rivers are less crowded. The gentlemen from the cities who came down for easy Mayfly fishing have climbed into their large cars and driven away. The river valleys have an air of luxurious peace and all through the long warm days, however bad the fishing may be, every fisherman can be buoyed up by the thought that the breathless excitement of the evening rise is still ahead.

Trying to catch trout under difficult summer conditions is something of a challenge. And success is all the more rewarding. At this time a dry fly may succeed in streams where wet flies usually reign supreme. Anyone fishing a downstream wet fly in low, clear water is likely to scare most of the trout long before they see his fly. But if he keeps low and casts a delicate dry fly to his trout from behind, he may get some well-deserved results.

Except on the chalk streams you will probably not see a great many trout rising in the heat of the day, but there are usually one or two. A few Pale Wateries should hatch even in the warmest weather, while cold rainy days may induce some Olives and Iron Blues to make an appearance. Sedges will be flying over the water and there may be enough of them to bring an odd trout splashing up to the surface.

Strange things may happen in summer. In August, ants may suddenly descend on the water and the trout may wake up to feed on them steadily. Artificial Red Ants are worth their place in a fly-box. Then, in the shade of a tree, a big trout may be waiting to feed on land-flies or bugs or beetles, or anything that drops from the leaves and branches. It is worth watching the water under trees carefully. These trout may not rise every minute, or even every five minutes, but they are frequently there and ready to be caught.

Spinners may visit the stream to lay their eggs at any time on a summer's day. But for most of it there may be little fly. Unless you are on a chalk stream you will 'fish the water' rather than 'fish the rise'. The trout have changed their positions since Spring. Rain-fed rivers look rather different now that the water-level has dropped. The deep, quiet pools still hold trout but they are mostly lazy, disinterested fish, since the water there tends to be staler and worse-oxygenated than in the faster shallows. The hungrier, more energetic fish will be in the shallow runs, or in the stickles, where the rippling water mixes with the air and absorbs some of its oxygen. In the evenings trout may rise all over the river.

In the still water of lakes and reservoirs, however, trout will forsake the shallows on hot days. They will seek really deep water—twenty feet down or over—because there, below the 'thermocline', the water-temperature is cooler. Until the evening, reservoir fishermen may not succeed with a dry fly.

Chalk-stream fishermen are much more fortunate in high summer than most. Olives, Iron Blues and Pale Wateries continue to hatch, somewhat spasmodically but not too badly. These chalk streams are spring-fed—they come welling up cool and clear from the chalk—and the level of them alters very little. The chalk downs act as a perpetual reservoir. The rivers may rise or fall a little but not nearly so much as the rain-fed streams. This means that floods and droughts are virtually unheard of. The temperature is more constant too. That is why water-cress, which flourishes in an even temperature, grows so well in Hampshire. Both trout and flies find the even temperature to their liking, so that although the days of July and August may be poor compared with those of earlier months, a chalk-stream fisherman can usually bargain on coming across feeding trout.

What can you reasonably expect from a good summer's day on a chalk stream? A great deal of fun. There is not only a chance of having one or two fish in the bag; there is also an immense variety in the number of different problems you meet during the day. The trout will seldom rise so well as they did in Spring but they will rise for a longer time each day and behave in more interesting ways. One of the charms of summer fishing is that every success is a small triumph. Earlier on you are really supposed to catch fish. You yourself imagine that you will, and all your friends imagine that you will. Your wife imagines that you will, too. If she begs for a brace for the pot and you fail her, you feel a worm. But now, if you fulfill the same duty, you're a hero indeed.

During the comparatively brief hatches of April it is practically impossible not to be keyed-up and a little nervous. In April, if you have no luck by the time the fly dwindles away, you become angry with yourself because you know you have missed your opportunities for the whole day. You incline to dash from one fish to the next. In July, however—when trout may be on the feed for longer hours—fishing can be less hurried. If you see a trout rising, you can take your time to approach him and to study his habits. If he defeats you, you can afford to look for another trout without haste, and if that one happens to defeat you as well you can always pin your hopes on a truly splendid evening rise.

Suppose, for instance, you arrive on the water about ten o'clock one morning? If you care to drag yourself out of bed you can of course arrive earlier, and in August you may well find good hatches of *Caenis* taking place at dawn and for a little time after. *Caenis* is the smallest member of the Ephemeropteran group of flies. A tiny stubby-winged insect, it may hatch out at any time from the end of May onwards but it is particularly likely to bring on a 'dawn rise' in August. Being so small, it is desperately hard to imitate. But occasionally trout will fall to a *Caenis* artificial or a little Houghton Ruby—or to something different but tempting such as a Caperer.

Ten o'clock is perhaps rather soon for there to be much other activity, but I do not think any fisherman ever regrets getting to his water with time to spare. Nothing is more upsetting than to arrive half-way through a rise, since then if you do not catch anything you have only yourself to blame for being so late. If you come early, before life on the river has really begun to move, this moment of arrival can be wonderfully pleasant. You make your way through the woods or through the meadows till quite suddenly you come upon the stream. There it is, your hunting ground for the whole day. You can hardly help being optimistic as you set up your rod in peace, sit down to await events and think to yourself: 'When the first trout rises, I expect he'll rise *there*'.

Another reward of arriving early is that although you may be very busy later in the day, now you can take time off to watch things going on all round. You can keep a solicitous eye on your favourite family of duck, as they swim in and out of the reeds, with the mother in the lead and children paddling themselves busily along behind her. Why is there always one ridiculous duckling who lags two or three yards behind all the rest and causes such tremendous trouble? Your day may be made by the rare flash of a kingfisher. Young pheasants, young moorhens (I don't like coots), young plovers and redshanks— all these will be about. And plenty of other birds and animals, including the water-rat. Or the water-vole, to give him his correct name. No river-scene is complete without an officious water-vole swimming from bank to bank, occasionally sitting up on a raft of weed to eat a reed-stem in his hands, just like a child eating a banana.

The river valley has a sleepy beauty in mid-summer. The lushness of the greens can become almost monotonous—but often the green of the cornfields is colourfully relieved by the red of poppies, the white of campion, or the yellow of mustard. In the water-meadows themselves there should be rosebay willow-herb, meadow-sweet, purple loosestrife, forget-me-nots and enough other plants to make a brave show.

Today, while you are waiting and watching and before any flies hatch, you see a trout start to feed on nymphs. At your feet is a green bed of ranunculus and by its side a golden patch of gravel. Suddenly a trout sidles out of the weed, lies on the gravel for a minute or two and then moves slowly upstream. Shortly afterwards there is a swirl on the surface, and after that another swirl several yards beyond, showing that the trout is taking nymphs on his way.

You consider trying to catch this trout on a nymph. Eventually you decide against the plan. It is always difficult to cast precisely for moving fish and all too often they play follow-my-leader with you. You may rush up-stream, casting every few yards, until they deceive you utterly by stopping still for a little so that you over-run them and put them down. Worse still, you may disturb several other fish. So you let this trout be. Early in the day it often does far more harm than good to charge up and down the river-bank before trout have started to feed properly. Patience may be a virtue here—though, contrary to popular belief, you seldom need much patience for dry-fly fishing. It is far too nerve-racking. Think of all the full-grown twelve-stone men you find shivering and quaking with fear behind a bush in case a half-pound trout should see them.

When you have waited another half-hour or so, a few Pale Wateries begin to hatch and the trout are not slow to take advantage of them. You try to choose a sizeable fish out of several who have now started to rise in full view. There is, after all, no sense at all in catching under-sized fish just for the sake of it—even though you may intend to return them to the water. Some may be so badly hooked that they have to be killed. And sometimes even lightly-hooked fish can be mortally damaged, particularly if the hook has caught hold in the tongue or gills. They may swim away and die later.

Two good trout are rising in mid-stream. You can guess they are large because they rise stolidly, confidently, without any of the splash that a small trout often makes when he comes up for a dun. They seem to displace a fair amount of water. Occasionally you catch a sight of their big, black nebs, which is a sure sign that they are not taking nymphs. The upper of the two fish looks slightly better, but if you cast for him first you will certainly put down the other. So you decide to start by attacking the lower one and hope to catch the pair of them.

At the third or fourth cast your Tups Indispensable lands in the right place. The trout surges up to it and you strike. There is a brief feeling of resistance, then a sickening slackness, and you see a turmoil in the water as the trout goes off to the dentist. Did you strike too soon? Did you pull the fly out of his jaws before he closed them and turned down? That seems the most likely answer. You determine not to make the same mistake twice, as you wait for the second of the two trout to show himself once more before you cast.

But, unfortunately, the second trout fails to rise again. The little flurry of Pale Watery has died away. Now the sun, coming out from behind a cloud, shines down upon a river that has suddenly become lifeless. It was a very short hatch. One or two young fish flop up spasmodically but they are too small and they are not rising steadily. You walk upstream and have a look round the next bend. Sure enough, there is a trout rising quietly in by the bank. The Tups Indispensable goes over him. He pays no attention to it.

You watch the trout for a little. Just because the Tup succeeded once, you cannot by any means guarantee that it will do so again. In summer there are so many different flies on the water throughout the day that two trout next door to each other may even be feeding on completely separate varieties. They may also change their diet from hour to hour, so that the only true guide is the evidence of the fisherman's own eyes at the time.

As you watch him the trout rises very gently, sipping down something that you cannot see. It might be spinner. Since you have noticed an occasional Olive Spinner on the water, you take a Lunn's Particular from your box and try it on the fish. This time there is no bungling. The trout takes it firmly and is well hooked. Then you realize, to your disappointment, that he is undersized after all. The trouble is that when trout rise to spinners a four-pounder may make just as tiny a dimple as a quarter-pound baby.

You guide the little fish to where you are standing, then you slide your fingers down the cast till they grasp the shank of the hook, and you wiggle it about in the water. The trout kicks off and swims away happily, never having left his native element. This is a good way of returning trout provided they are not severely hooked.

Just upstream are some shallows, where you think you may find a fish. There does not seem to be very much happening but you can clearly see one medium-sized trout hovering over a patch of gravel between two weed-beds, obviously on the look-out for fly. He rises once almost immediately, making a scarcely discernible break in the rough water. Several Medium Olives are hatching so you tie on a Hare's Ear and offer it to the trout. He takes it—you strike—the hook goes home—and the fish dashes downstream to bury himself in a dense clump of weed at your feet. (Many fish work their way a few yards upstream from their homes to feed, and when they are hooked their first thought is 'Home, James', so they usually make their first run downstream.) You try hand-lining this trout and it works. He comes clear of the weeds and after a little more excitement you land your first sizeable fish of the day.

He weighs about a pound and a quarter. As you continue upstream afterwards you nearly walk on top of another trout. You suddenly catch sight of his tail. The tail is sticking out from under a patch of floating weed. As you watch you can see the trout move out into the stream and almost immediately move back to his hiding-place under the weed. Here is a trout who is lying in shelter but also keeping an eye out for passing nymphs or shrimps. Perhaps a Pheasant Tail nymph, passing down by the side of the weed-bed, might tempt him?

You make a cast—either a good one or a lucky one. Out comes the trout. You tighten—and yes, you have him on. Thank goodness, he makes for the open water and three minutes later one more sizeable fish is in the net. This trout was an unexpected catch, and you might easily never have noticed him. During the summer, when there are no big hatches of fly, it is well worth-while scanning every bit of the riverbed that you can see. You may find trout who can be induced to feed. A motionless trout glued to the bottom will seldom take anything, but a trout that appears alive and active—especially if he is poised in mid-water or near the surface—may grab a sunk nymph or come up for a floating fly. A big sedge or Caperer sometimes does the job. The important thing, of course, is to see these trout before you are so close to them that they take fright.

By now it is two o'clock. Two sizeable fish, one undersized fish, and one fish pricked. Not too bad. While you are wondering whether any more fresh fly will hatch it starts to rain and a few duns re-appear on the water. The trout start rising again. This time the rise lasts a little longer and there are Medium Olives on the water for about three-quarters of an hour. During this hatch you lose one trout and catch another sizeable one, only just over a pound but a nice plump fish. Since you have a brace already, you put him back carefully. Before the rise peters out, you also manage to miss a couple of good fish.

A hundred years further on, a trout is steadily sip-sip-sipping under an old tree overhanging some smooth water. The sky has now cleared and as the trout moves into a shaft of sunlight you can see his black shape. He is undoubtedly a big trout. Perhaps he is taking spinner? There do not seem to be any spinner on the water but you try the trout with a Houghton Ruby, a Pheasant Tail and a Tup. None of them interest him at all so you decide that he must be feeding on smut and that a Black Gnat may catch him.

You show him a tiny Black Gnat and a little hump appears on the surface near your fly as the trout comes up to inspect it, then refuses it and goes down again. That was a close shave. You present the Black Gnat to him a second time but he takes no more notice of it, nor can he be attracted by any of your other small flies. He goes on rising persistently. In desperation you knot on a large Caperer. Almost before it reaches him he dashes at it like a tiger. In great surprise and completely off your guard, you strike badly, prick him hard and see him flounder on the top of the water for a couple of seconds before the hook loses its hold. A shame. Despite the difference in size, smutting trout do sometimes take Caperers very readily. Perhaps the juicy bulk of these large flies makes them look good mouthfuls to a trout working hard at small insects.

As you walk back downstream you see a trout's tail waving like a banner above the surface of the river. The trout has his nose buried deep in some weed and is literally standing on his head as he searches for shrimp. You put a Pope's Nondescript over him, choosing one of the intervals when he takes his head out of the weeds. A Pope's Nondescript, says Skues, will occasionally catch a tailing trout. This does not seem to be one of the occasions. The trout never even looks at your fly so you leave him to his acrobatics and continue down-stream.

The river looks fairly dead now. Flies and fish are both taking a rest. But at about four-thirty some spinners begin coming down on the water. You can see them as they are carried along by the quiet current, and their red bodies and white wings show that they are Iron Blue spinners. So onto the end of your cast goes a Houghton Ruby. Meanwhile, a fish has started to rise every twenty seconds or so under the far bank. Your Houghton Ruby drops over there. Another rise and you strike. This time a rather larger trout forges upstream, playing deep and heavy, so that you have to follow him.

After two minutes of playing you still have not caught a glimpse of your trout. You think he must be big. He is not taking out much line but when he does he takes it out without any effort at all and he feels really solid. He might be any size. After another minute he comes in under your own bank and you see him to be a thick fish of at least two pounds. He sees you at the same time, which sends him off on another headlong tour of the stream. Will you never land him? He tires slowly, and then you slide the net under him, praying fervently that you will not lose him at the last moment as he thrashes around on the surface. All goes well, luckily, and after a little heart-searching you decide he is too much of a trophy to release. Your spring-balance tells you he weighs three pounds.

While the spinners are still falling you catch another undersized trout. This one, unfortunately, is not nearly so lightly hooked as the first one and you cannot release him without lifting him onto the bank. Here is the way to do it. Before handling him at all you wet your hands carefully so as not to rub off any of the slime that protects his skin. Then, when he is on the bank, you try to ease the hook out tenderly to avoid tearing his mouth. The process takes quite a little while and when you replace him in the water he starts to turn belly upwards. If the stream carries him away in such a state he may get into trouble, so you hold him in the water with his head upstream till he regains his breath, wriggles out of your hand and goes off to recuperate in a weed-bed.

By the time you have finished doing this it is nearly six o'clock and the spinner-rise is over. The stream will probably stay quiet now until the evening rise starts. You can go home with a clear conscience to have some supper before coming back to fish again an hour or so before sunset. As for lunch, you have probably taken the opportunity of a lull in the fishing to eat some sandwiches—if you remembered them. Pocketable sandwiches are a great blessing to fishermen. Set meals are a great curse. If you are expected back at your host's house or any other meeting-place for a cooked lunch you can be quite certain the trout will begin rising at that very hour. Good hosts and good landlords have usually learned through bitter experience that fishing guests are rather erratic time-keepers.

Today has been a very good day, with its four sizeable fish. It has not, however, been quite exceptional. There has been great variety in it and continual hope all day long. I myself do rather like to catch trout when I go fishing. (One looks such an idiot if one doesn't.) But even if I only catch one sizeable fish on a summer's day I am always very glad that I did not stay at home to wait for the evening rise.

CHAPTER 11

Pause for Reflection

By now the bulk of our season is a cherished memory. But it is not yet
over and the end of it is highly likely to treat us handsomely. This is a
good time, perhaps, while in stray moments of leisure we sit and
count the all days still ahead of us, to reflect also on the days behind
that have passed so fleetingly. Can we be proud of the performance
we put up during those days?

There are—or at any rate there should be—two separate sides of
that performance to mull over in our minds. First there is of course
the obvious side. Have we managed to fish reasonably well, better
than we did last season? And then there is a less obvious side that can
nevertheless rank equally high in our assessment of ourselves as
fishermen. If it does not do so now, it certainly will eventually. Have
we behaved towards our quarry with all the care and respect
undoubtedly due to it?

The chances are that we shall start with the obvious. We shall
simply try to appraise the progress of our ability to catch more trout.
We shall relive with some self-satisfaction those moments of splendid
triumph that made us confident we were fishing more and more
skilfully. We shall relive, too, the pitiful anguish of our many failures
and of all the occasions when memorable trout defeated us, often
because of our own inefficiency. We shall probably make resolves to
improve certain inadequacies and to rid ourselves of certain bad
habits that we now realise have crept up on us.

A self-critical survey such as this often bears fruit very quickly, so
it is well worth carrying out at fairly frequent intervals during the
season. But now let us turn to the rather less material side of things
and review our whole attitude and behaviour towards the trout we
pursue. It is perhaps high time that we gave a thought to this. Apart

from a few references to showing consideration towards undersized fish, I have so far hardly touched on it.

Yet the fact is that the way in which we regard and treat our quarry is very far from being a remote or trivial detail. More and more as the years go by, it has a tremendous influence on just how much pleasure and pride we derive from our fishing. It will tend to govern our esteem both of the sport and of ourselves as people who enjoy it. It will also, incidentally, affect the opinion that non-fishermen have of fishing in general, something to which we should certainly pay good heed for the sake of the future, perhaps especially in these days of increasing concern for non-human life. So please forgive me if I now try to express my own viewpoint about it.

The one phrase 'respect for the quarry' seem to sum most of it up. I first heard the phrase myself from that great actor and fisherman Sir Michael Hordern (though he says he may not have originated it) and have clung to it as a guideline ever since. It seems to crystallise so many of the feelings we should have and the measures we should take whenever we go fishing.

Few trout fishermen will deny that the trout is an exceptionally noble quarry, a quarry deserving of respect. Nor will they deny that the very best way of showing respect is to try to see that not a single trout suffers any unnecessary pain or (since some scientists believe that fish feel little in the way of pain) any unnecessary distress. That of course is why we ought not to cast deliberately to undersized fish, a point already stressed in the last chapter. To catch a trout that we know must be immediately returned—if he is not too badly hooked—shows him no kindness at all. It reduces the trout, in fact, to being little more than a mere plaything, which does him no honour whatsoever.

Just the same principle of being as merciful as we can naturally applies whenever we unhook a trout we wish to put back. And yet some fairly nauseating sights are sadly enough not too uncommon when some fishermen attempt it. One or two of the worst sort, for whom sheer ignorance can be the only possible excuse, can sometimes be seen lifting a trout straight from the water, tearing the hook with a single movement from his throat and then throwing him back into the river with a noisy splash, there to float on downstream belly-upwards till he dies. Most fishermen, thank goodness, are far less callous—but many of them, nevertheless, are obviously unaware of

9. BRIAN CLARKE hooks a fish on the Wiltshire Avon. As the photograph shows, he has struck without any undue force or vehemence. The word 'tighten' describes the right action far more successfully than the word 'strike'.

10. A WISE FISHERMAN, as this photograph demonstrates, always keeps as low as possible when approaching a wary trout. He will also make use of all the available cover he can find. The photo is of John Goddard – a wise and first-rate fisherman by any standard. The scene is the Test not far above Romsey.

11. WADING IS OFTEN USEFUL but perhaps few apprentice fishermen realise just how important it is to wade as gently and quietly and slowly as possible. Careless, heavy-footed wading causes vibrations that will frighten trout at a considerable distance. Charles Jardine, photographed here on the Wiltshire Avon, needs no such warning. He always wades cautiously, and as the picture shows, is usually rewarded for it.

all the precautions they can and really should take to help a released trout to survive. Here they are in full:

1 If you hook a fish that you think you will wish to return, play him hard and bring him in just as quickly as possible. The less exhausted he is when you unhook him, the safer he will be.
2 Always try to keep a fish underwater while you take out the hook. If you can do it without even touching him, simply by taking hold of the shank of the hook with a forefinger and thumb, so much the better.
3 Never, however, jag at the hook at all hard, though you may often have to use both hands to avoid doing so. Then hold the trout gently in one hand, still keeping him underwater, while you work on the hook with the other.
4 You may sometimes find it virtually impossible to extract the hook without being able to see exactly where it is. In those cases it is better to lift the trout from the water rather than just wrench at the hook blindly. But make sure that your hands are wet first, since dry hands can remove some of the protective slime that covers a trout's body.
5 When you hold a trout out of water, hold him upside down—belly-up, that is. It is a strange but true fact, and not a very well-known one either, that trout struggle a good deal less when held like this. And of course the less they struggle, the less they harm themselves.
6 Although I have spoken of using fingers and thumbs, you should really carry something with you which happens to be a far better instrument for unhooking trout. This is a pair of 'surgical forceps', known in America as a 'haemostat'. They will give you an infinitely firmer and safer grip of the hook and can be bought at almost any tackle-shop.
7 Once your trout is unhooked you must satisfy yourself beyond all doubt that he can take care of himself before you let him go. If you have managed to unhook him quickly underwater with one hand, he may make off immediately with a flick of his tail. Then he is all right. But if you have used both hands and taken some time over the job of unhooking him, he may well need reviving. If he has been out of the water, he certainly will.
8 To revive a trout simply hold him in the water and make certain (if you are fishing a river rather than a stillwater) that he faces upstream. If he faces downstream he cannot breathe. Hold him there till he wriggles vigorously enough to escape your hand and swim away. At the outset he may seem almost lifeless and try to turn belly-up. But do not despair of him. So long as his mouth and gills are still opening and closing, he has plenty of hope. I have sometimes spent as long as ten minutes reviving a trout fully—with eventual success.

9 Even when the trout swims away, do not abandon him just yet. If you can see him, watch him for a few moments. If he has vanished into a weed-bed or into deep water, watch the area where he may be. Once in a while you may find that he is not so fit as you—and perhaps he too—imagined. If you see him in any apparent difficulty, use your net to bring him in again and revive him completely. Although this may very seldom be necessary, it is well worth spending a brief moment or so to be certain your released trout is in good shape.

10 If a trout bleeds at the mouth while you unhook him, especially from the tongue or gills, he has hardly any chance of survival. It is kindest to use your priest on him straight away.

A healthy trout is in fact a very tough gentleman. He can sometimes recover comparatively easily from wounds or experiences that might well be thought quite enough to put an end to him. But not all trout are in perfect health, particularly in stocked waters, and in any case a trout's natural resilience is no excuse whatever for not unhooking him as carefully and humanely as possible.

Now this brings us on to an alternative way of making sure that every trout can be returned with the absolute minimum of harm or discomfort. It is the best way of all, by far the best way. Fish for him with a dry fly tied on a barbless hook. Then you will find that wherever the hook has lodged in his mouth, you can simply slide it out with no trouble at all. You will save yourself all the agony of wrestling with hooks that happen to be deeply embedded, and of wondering whether the fish can ever be set free to continue living. No wonder barbless hooks are nowadays becoming more and more popular.

But will you not then lose a great many fish while playing them? Perhaps surprisingly, the truth is that you will lose comparatively few. Provided you keep a taut line between yourself and the trout for as much of the time as possible, as indeed you always should, the fish will usually remain quite safely hooked. If he dives into a weed-bed, that may be another matter. But a trout that goes to weed is often lost anyway, whether the hook has a barb or not.

This is not of course to say that you will lose no trout at all on account of using a barbless hook. But a barbless hook does have another advantage which compensates for this. When you use an ordinary hook, the barb constitutes a very slight obstruction to its penetration, especially into the harder parts of a trout's mouth. This is sometimes why you only prick a trout when he rises to you and you strike. A barbless hook can be 'set' in the trout's mouth more easily and more often.

A well-known American fisherman recently carried out a little statistical survey of his own on barbed versus barbless hooks. Over a period of time he found that when he used a barbless hook he lost 6% more fish than when he used a barbed one. But as against this he hooked 20% more of the fish he rose. As you can imagine, he now only uses barbless hooks.

It is also humane to use barbless hooks for one reason quite apart from trouble-free unhooking. When you play a trout on a barbless hook you usually find yourself playing him pretty hard, simply for fear that the hook may come out at any moment. So you bring him in all the sooner, in a less exhausted state. His ordeal will be shorter and his chances of survival excellent.

Some tackle-shops sell flies on barbless hooks, but as yet they are few and far between. This need present no problem at all, however. Simply take a normal fly and flatten the barb with a pair of flat-nosed pliers or some perfectly ordinary tweezers. You will break off the point of the barb while you do this and a small hump will be left on the hook instead. This hump is in fact a great asset. Compared with a completely smooth barbless hook, its grip in the trout's mouth is a little safer. Yet you will still be able to slide the hook out just as easily.

Obviously it stands to reason that if you wish to kill a trout you should do so with no delay at all. Never leave him gasping on the bank while you search for a rock or stone or stick to use on him. Always carry a priest for the purpose. Alternatively, if the trout you catch are not too large to hold firmly in one hand, a single sharp knock on the handle of your landing-net is often quicker still. It will save the few precious seconds you may spend fumbling for your priest, at a time when every second counts.

The word 'kill' is one that more and more fishermen seem to avoid these days, entirely instinctively. And quite rightly too. It has a certain unfeeling ring to it that is hardly in keeping with the nature of the sport. Books written a generation ago often speak of 'killing' a brace of trout. Nowadays they are far more likely to speak of 'taking' or 'catching' or 'keeping' a brace of trout.

And this of course raises wider issues. To what extent do we really wish, or should we really wish, to kill as many trout as we can? The urge is very understandable in a beginner. He still has to prove that he can catch plenty of trout. But it is not so understandable, nor so forgiveable, when it overcomes more mature fishermen and turns them into mere 'killers', as the most merciless ones are sometimes called. (In America they are often described as 'meat fishermen'!) Fishing is after all far more than just a manner of killing fish. A great deal of the pleasure lies simply in deceiving them, but there is more to it than that as well. The motto of The Flyfishers' Club runs: 'There's more to fishing than catching fish'. It is as true a motto as a club could possibly have.

You will seldom see a genuinely mature fisherman rushing frantically from place to place and casting without pause in the hope of catching and killing as many trout as possible. He will take his day in an infinitely more leisurely way, giving himself plenty of time to sit and watch the river, the countryside, the wildlife. He will be more relaxed and will enjoy himself all the more because of it. His demands on the stock of trout in his stream will probably be moderate. If he catches several fish he may well keep only as many as his family tells him they need for food, returning all the others.

Some policy or other of moderation does seem to be very much in tune with the spirit of flyfishing. Unfortunately there are many stillwaters where it simply cannot be applied, since their rules forbid you to return any of the fish you catch. And again there are some fishermen, happily a minority, who seem to find moderation un-welcome. On good days they forget the motto of the Flyfishers' Club and instead follow their own favourite motto of 'make hay while the sun shines', often bringing back more fish than they know what to do with. Some of them may even have to be thrown away. This, of course, shows complete disrespect for them. Every one of those trout will have died unnecessarily.

Bag-limits naturally enforce a degree of moderation. But you may feel that moderation should really not have to be enforced. There is one other motto that I admire very much, the motto of the Federation of Fly Fishers in America. It says: 'Don't catch your limit—limit your catch'.

But most good American trout–fishermen, and many Europeans as well, go further still. They fish according to the 'catch-and-release' code and return every single trout to the water, every single one. (Unless he has been too badly hooked, of course.)

Does this sound a surprising way of taking part in a field-sport? If you read the game-fishing magazines in this country, you will find the whole issue of catch-and-release being constantly debated, usually pretty hotly. Some fishermen are for it. Some are against it. So let me try to put the arguments for both sides, since each of us has to make up our own mind about it. There is no 'must' involved and no 'mustn't'.

Traditionally we in Britain have always thought of fishing as part and parcel of 'hunting' in the overall sense of the word. And again traditionally, a good and successful 'hunt' customarily ends with a 'kill' that usually serves some useful purpose, perhaps the culling of foxes, perhaps the provision of meat. In this latter instance the final and rightful reward of the hunter is an enjoyable meal.

If you take away this element, it can perhaps be said that you prevent fishing from being a true field-sport. That thought was admirably expressed to me recently by a keen fisherwoman with whom I was discussing catch-and-release. 'It's positively decadent', she said. 'If you put back all the fish you catch, you've taken a sport and turned it into a game.'

Furthermore the atavistic instinct of the hunt is deeply embedded in most of us. That late and great fisherman Dick Walker used frequently to say: 'For every year that Man has been farming on this planet, he has hunted for ninety-nine years'. He was quite right. So if one likes trout to eat, why not claim the hunter's due reward for skill?

Nor need it be any sign of disrespect to kill a quarry, provided it is done quickly. On the contrary, since time beyond telling hunters have shown not only respect but even veneration towards the animals they killed and ate. Cave-drawings indicate this clearly. And on the other side of the world some primitive African tribes, when they have made a kill, still perform a ritual dance of gratitude and reverence before the carcass, thanking it for having saved them yet again from starvation. This may seem a little far removed from our fishing discussion, but I think it has a bearing on it.

Now for the other side of the argument. The concept of catch-and-release began in America as a conservation measure. The idea of it was to preserve as far as possible the head of wild trout in certain American streams, and so to rely a great deal less on stocked fish.

This was very important in America at the time. Nearly all water is public there, open to anyone who has a fishing licence, and the stocking of it is the responsibility of the relevant state. Then as now, some streams were pretty crowded and on some of them flyfishing was fast becoming something of a farce. Everyone waited till a stocking took place. Then a whole crowd of fishermen descended on the spot. All the newly introduced, innocent trout were caught within two or three days, after which the river was left denuded and simply not worth fishing till the date of the next stocking—when of course everything was re-enacted exactly as before. This sort of fishing had a name to itself—it was called 'chasing the hatchery truck'.

Only experimentally at the outset, certain stretches of water were designated as 'no-kill' stretches, where the rule was that every trout should be returned. Naturally there were a good many fears about the experiment and exactly the same fears are now being voiced about catch-and-release in this country. But American experience has proved them baseless.

Perhaps the biggest fear is—will large numbers of released trout die anyway? The answer is 'No', always given that they are not badly handled. A fairly recent survey in Yellowstone Park (Montana, USA) showed that all the trout in the water studied had been caught on average no fewer than seven times. The proportion of them failing to survive was even lower than once imagined—a mere 0.3%. These were cut-throat trout, but there is no reason at all to think that brown or rainbow trout would have a more difficult time of it.

Then another fear is this. Once trout have been caught once or twice on a dry fly, will they be reluctant to continue feeding on surface food? Again the answer seems to be a most definite No. The no-kill stretches of American rivers—and these have multiplied considerably since the experimental days—are now often if not usually by far the most popular stretches. This is simply because they contain many more free-rising trout than do other stretches, from which fish have been removed and killed. It is true that whenever a trout is released he becomes just a little harder to deceive next time. Most good American fishermen, however, enjoy the challenge of this a great deal more than they enjoy fishing for freshly-stocked, easy-to-catch trout.

So by and large the scheme has been successful in helping the preservation of wild trout, sometimes to the extent that stocking is no longer needed, and also in improving the fishing on many streams.

But there is another side to catch-and-release as well. Many American friends of mine have become so used to releasing trout that quite apart from any conservation motives, they now find it distasteful to kill them. If they fish with me over here, even in places where it is customary to keep a few trout, they put all theirs back. On grounds of humanity alone, they say they prefer to see a good trout swim happily away than to bludgeon it on the noddle.

Not all American fishermen fish on the catch-and-release principle, far from it. But very nearly all the best ones do, as well as the best-known ones. Catch-and-release has also spread, though not on the same scale, to many European countries such as France and Belgium. We in Britain have been slower than most to take it up, probably for the reasons mentioned earlier and perhaps also because we have so little public water. Plenty of British fishermen disapprove of it—and I would certainly never decry them for it. But even so and even here, the idea of catch-and-release seems to be gaining just a little ground each year, though very gradually indeed, and nowadays some of our more notable trout fishermen (John Goddard and Brian Clarke, to name only two) seldom or never choose to keep any of the trout they catch.

So I wonder what you think? Personally I would never dream of trying to dictate to anyone on the issue. I feel it is a matter about which every individual should form his or her own opinion. But perhaps it is only right for me to say where I stand myself. While I do this, however, you may find it useful to remember that I have now fished long enough to quell nearly all the blood-lust that I am sure I had in my younger days, not that I was in any way proud of it.

I am in favour of a great deal more catch-and-release being practised in this country than at present, at any rate wherever it stands a chance of fulfilling its original intention—to preserve and increase the head of wild trout in a river. It can also reduce stocking costs and so make the fishing a little cheaper for the many fishermen not quite fortunate enough to be able to shell out five-pound notes by the hundred.

Now that is not to say that I believe catch-and-release can ever eliminate stocking in heavily-fished waters. But, together with other necessary steps, it can indeed improve the balance between wild and farmed trout. The other steps should include making the river as suitable as possible for wild trout, particularly as regards good spawning beds, and also seeing that the trout stocked are no larger than the natural size for the river. It is often a good notion, too, to stock with plenty of yearlings each year, as well as with sizeable fish, since the yearlings will be indistinguishable from wild trout by the time they mature.

Nor do I mean to imply that a stocked trout need necessarily be a quarry to be sneezed at, provided he has been in the river for a while. But the wild trout, in my opinion, is the best quarry of all and the tragedy is that he has become very hard to find in many famous Southern waters. One of the reasons is over-stocking. To satisfy the demands of fishermen, some of whom are inevitably 'killers', many stretches are stocked far too lavishly, far too frequently, and with trout so large that a wild trout has no chance of competing with them. The fishing then becomes child's play. Is there really much true 'hunting' involved when you kill easy trout which may well have been put there just a day or two beforehand, so that you can catch them without too much trouble?

This is why I should have no hesitation in welcoming more catch-and-release, as one possible way of reversing a process that has turned parts of our finest rivers into little more than 'running-water stewponds'. But having said that, I must make a confession. The waters I fish myself could never be described as running-water stewponds and I cannot always maintain that I behave on them as a completely wholehearted catch-and-releaser should.

I happen to think that trout are delicious to eat. So I do sometimes keep (if I can catch them) any fish that my wife says she needs for the pot. I may also occasionally keep a brace for good friends. But the trout that I catch over and above these invariably go back—undamaged, I hope, since I nearly always use barbless hooks. I manage to resist all temptation to fill our deep-freeze. And I try to return every wild trout I catch, keeping only those that I can tell to be stocked fish.

So if you wish, you can justly criticise me for being ambivalent. Whenever I fish in America, however, a startling change comes over me. I immediately find myself feeling precisely as my American hosts do. I put back all the trout I catch without thinking for a second of any good meals I may be missing. And from the very outset I discover that it would most certainly shame and repel me to kill a single one of them. Catch-and-release becomes the only natural and pleasant way to fish. It is a far easier habit to acquire than one might imagine—and

I believe I might well end up feeling rather prouder of myself if I practised it a bit more consistently in this country.

I hope that these random reflections may have provided just a little food for thought. But now let us finish our season.

CHAPTER 12

The End of it All

September is a good month for fishermen, albeit a sad one in ways. The days are much shorter now, and the thought that autumn is waiting impatiently to blow the green leaves away makes every hour more precious. The season is drawing to its close, but gloriously so. The fields have turned from green to gold, and although the noon sun seems almost as warm as ever, it is no longer the thick, sultry heat of August. Wispy mists cover the countryside in the early morning, and on the way to the river, the sun shimmers through myriads of starry, dewy spider-threads strung from leaf to leaf and reed to reed. And, if the spiders are busy and active during September, the trout are often no less so.

While fishermen make the most of their last few weeks of the season, the trout may be equally keen to make the most of good feeding before they start to spawn. Then they will feed very little. As soon as their spawning activities begin, food ceases to interest them so much. In any case there is not nearly so much food to be had in the winter months. So while the food is available, and while they are hungry, they feed well.

September, whatever the weather, is nearly always better than August. Fishing may begin to pick up in the last week of August, if plenty of Black Gnats appear on the water. Black Gnats are rather uncertain creatures. Unlike Olives and Iron Blues, which hatch in fair numbers every year, Black Gnats may arrive in millions one year, to be practically absent the next. May is a good month for them. After that there are very few to be seen till about August 20th. Then for a fortnight, the Black Gnat season can occasionally provide really splendid fishing, with as many fish rising as during the Mayfly.

This may only happen in one year out of many. But that year is worth waiting for. The common Black Gnat—a *Bibio* type—hatches on land and lays its eggs on land. It is not really a water-fly at all, and you do not have a proper 'hatch' of Black Gnats. It only falls on the water by mistake, or when it is dead. So there has to be a tremendous quantity of Black Gnats about, before enough can fall on the river to bring the trout up. And, in a good year for Black Gnats, there are swarms of them about. They cover the plants by the side of the water, particularly all the white 'umbrella' plants. Whenever you notice that these plants are hardly white any longer, but almost black with the tiny insects, you can bank on a very good day's fishing.

The day may start in a normal way, with a few trout feeding on Pale Wateries or Medium Olives, or on their spinners. Then the Black Gnats will begin to fall. The important thing here is to change to a Black Gnat quickly, however keen fish may have seemed to take other flies beforehand. While they are feeding on Black Gnats they will seldom take anything else. The insects on the plants will have provided some warning of what to expect, and the Black Gnats themselves are quite easy to see on the smoother parts of the stream. They look like small, dark-coloured bundles. As they are usually dead or dying, and cannot escape, the trout take them steadily and quietly, without any fuss at all.

Falls of Black Gnat are seldom continuous throughout the day. They may commence at any time from eleven o'clock onwards. After a fall there may be a lull, when only an occasional Black Gnat floats down, and then a little later the surface will again be speckled with them. They often float downstream in clusters. During the lulls, the trout may revert to other flies, or stop rising until the next fall. The trout always seem to love Black Gnats, provided there are plenty of them, and the falls may go on intermittently until three or four o'clock.

Most stretches of water have one or two dead bits where hardly any trout ever seem to rise. This is often because the river-bed has become silted-up there, and very few flies like it. But Black Gnats are an exception. They drop down more or less at random all over the valley, and as many will drop on the poor bits of the river as on the better fly-bearing bits. So if the Black Gnats appear in strength, it is often worth visiting dead water, which will probably have been fished very little indeed. You may easily pick up a big old bottom-feeding trout, who would not dream of letting you find him on the surface at any time other than this, and perhaps in the Mayfly season.

A tying of a double Black Gnat, which is an imitation of two flies mating, can be very useful sometimes. The insects often sink down onto the water while paired together. The Black Gnats last well into September, and trout can sometimes be caught on them half-way through the month. Then, as soon as they die away, the other flies begin to hatch more regularly than they did in the heat of summer. The September hatches may make the season end with a bang, not a whimper. Pale Wateries will still be there, and more Medium Olives will hatch as the weather grows cooler. Towards the end of the month, a few Large Dark Olives may appear on the water again, for the first time since Spring. In October these flies hatch nearly every day, and they carry on throughout the winter, which means that although the fisherman only sees them for a brief period at the beginning and end of his season, they are really one of the commonest flies on most rivers.

Spinners, too, will be in evidence throughout the day and especially in the early evening. These September days are comparatively short, and all the more active because of it. There is no long lull between the daytime rise and the evening rise, as there is in July. Sometimes the two rises almost dovetail into each other, with scarcely a pause, so that you can fish solidly all day. You can have supper at a respectable hour too—after having fished the evening rise.

The trout in the river will be in good condition and they may even be ripe. When you clean them, you may find them heavy with milt or large eggs. But trout may not be the only fish in the water. There may be grayling as well. These, with their big dorsal fins, will be very fit now. You can look upon the silver grayling as either a game fish or a coarse fish, according to the way you feel about him. Grayling have big scales like many coarse fish. Their lips look better for sucking up food from the bottom than for feeding like a trout. Yet they take flies on the surface readily. They have none of the trout's colouring, but their adipose fins show that they originally came from the same family as trout and salmon. The adipose fin is the tiny, stumpy, useless fin between the big dorsal fin and the tail fin. It is supposed to be a remnant of the far-off days when all fish had one huge fin running the whole length of their backs. All the members of the salmon family have hung onto this last vestige of it.

Grayling, like coarse fish and unlike trout, spawn in the Spring. If you have any grayling in your river, you see them cavorting about on their spawning grounds as you are beginning your season's trout-fishing. You do not catch many of them then, because they take little interest in food while they are spawning. One or two, however, usually the small ones who have not yet begun to spawn, will always rise. The others wait till mid-May or June, and then begin to show themselves properly. On some rivers, where conditions suit them well, grayling are the fly-fisherman's chief quarry and they have their own legal season from June 16th till March 14th. They were first introduced to the chalk streams some time ago to provide fly-fishing during the Autumn for people who hated to put their rods away at the end of September. Unfortunately, however, they multiplied too fast for anyone's liking and now they are treated there as vermin—because they eat up the trout's food. To protect the trout, water-keepers and fishermen catch, net, electrocute and hunt the unfortunate grayling all the year round.

No-one can be blamed for doing this in an effort to improve expensive trout waters. But even so, I regard the grayling as a game fish. Admittedly, it is disappointing to catch a grayling when you expect a trout, but the grayling has much to be said in his favour. His chief virtue is that he rises freely and constantly. In the sweltering heat of a summer or early September afternoon, when too few flies are on the water to attract the lazy trout, grayling are nearly always prepared to rise. Whatever the flies may be, smuts or duns or spinners, they seem to whet a grayling's appetite.

Grayling do not rise in quite the same way as trout. Whereas a feeding trout likes to lie just below the surface, so that he can tilt up to take a fly with the minimum of effort, a grayling soars up to grab flies from a much deeper level, often from the river-bed itself. They are far quicker than trout and can often beat trout to a fly. Just as a trout is preparing to take a fly, in his own steady way, you may see a grayling dash up from below to steal it from him.

Another result of the grayling's swiftness is that he is very difficult to hook when you strike. First, he sometimes misses the fly in his haste. Second, if the fisherman strikes with the usual deliberation that he finds necessary for trout, he is often too late for grayling. I have seen many expert fishermen, who would scarcely ever fail to hook a trout, having their confidence in striking torn into shreds by missing grayling after grayling. I think one inevitably misses a great many grayling, the only saving feature being that one usually has another chance at them. They are less easily put off the rise than trout, and after a grayling has been missed, he may easily rise again to the same fly three or four times, until you eventually succeed in hooking him.

When trout are rising and when you would rather cast for trout than grayling, it is useful to be able to distinguish between the rises of the two fish. Unfortunately mistakes are only too common. If, however, several fish are all rising together in a small area, they are more likely to be grayling than trout, because grayling live in shoals while trout never do. If you catch sight of a tail above the water as the fish dives down, particularly a forked tail, it will probably be a grayling-rise, since grayling have forked tails which often break the surface as they turn sharply downwards. Grayling, on the whole, rise more splashily than trout. And they are less shy about rising in the open, in fact they seem to prefer it. A fish feeding under a bank, therefore, or right up against a weed-bed, is liable to be a trout.

When there is very little fly, and hardly a trout rising, the grayling can provide excellent substitute sport. And when the trout season is over, grayling fishing is by any standard a fine sport in its own right. It takes an arrant snob with quite the wrong values to disdain grayling fishing, and I am sorry for fishermen who do. Grayling make good eating, too. If you scale them—or better still, skin them—they will be all the tastier. It is one of the great advantages of flyfishing that the old epithet 'the unspeakable in pursuit of the uneatable' cannot be applied to it.

Grayling like much the same flies as do trout, though they are probably not so discriminating. They can always be caught on an imitation of the fly that is hatching. But they can also be lured by a flash of colour, and a bright fly like a Red Tag is very successful for them. Sometimes even bigger bags are caught during Autumn from chalk streams on the wet fly—or more probably on a nymph such as Sawyer's Killer Bug—when the trout season is over. Grayling can grow fairly heavy. Two-pounders are not rare on the chalk streams. A normal adult grayling is about the same size as an adult trout. The record grayling, however, stands at only seven pounds and two ounces. Grayling differ from their cousins in that they seldom feed on the smaller fish that go to nourish great trout.

One thought that may (and should) pass through the fisherman's mind in September is water-improvement. What can be done to make the fishing better before next April? In good trout waters with natural spawning grounds—always provided the waters have not been over-fished—the trout should be able to look after themselves. After all, they have done so for thousands of years. But very many waters nowadays *are* fished more heavily than is good for them, and you cannot take out hundreds of trout every year without giving the fish-population a helping hand to restore the balance.

Should you, for instance, stock with young trout? And if so, how young should they be? A sizeable trout, reared to maturity, is more likely to survive when he is put into the river than a younger one, but then he is more expensive to buy. At the other end of the scale, it is possible to stock with trout-eggs or fry, provided suitable nurseries have been prepared in the water. Ideally, these should be clean, gravelly side-streams carefully protected by grids and wire from birds, pike and other trout-enemies. The young trout can be released into the main river when they are old enough to look after themselves properly. This is a cheap way of stocking, but many of the eggs and the young trout will die. Between these two extremes, yearlings can be really excellent trout to stock—especially since they grow up to be just like wild trout.

But none of these stocked trout, at whatever age they are introduced, will live and grow unless conditions in the river or lake are first made right for them. If there is too little oxygen or if there are too few good lies, they will die or go elsewhere if they can. If there is too little food, the big fish will become lanky, while the small trout will either starve or remain as dwarfs. Again, if the water is infested by pike or coarse fish, the trout stand little chance.

Once the water is put right, your trout will thrive, and you may even be able to give up the idea of stocking altogether. With the right conditions, Nature herself provides the best and cheapest way of producing trout, and will produce as many as the food in the river will support. Of course, where no spawning-beds exist, or where the water is so frequently fished that too few trout are left at the season's end to make up for the season's losses, owners have no choice and are forced to stock every year. Reservoirs, too, usually have inadequate spawning grounds and rely on the 'put and take' form of fishing—that is, you get out what you put in. Or to be more precise, you get out at least a percentage of what you put it.

Regular stocking is an essential policy for many a good fishery. And after a few weeks in the water, stocked trout will become as shy and difficult to catch as wild ones. Nevertheless, there are many fishermen who would rather catch a half-pound wild trout than a three-pound rainbow who started life in a trout-farm. Both sorts of trout have their place in the scheme of things, and we should not disparage either of them.

Food, oxygen, good lies, clean spawning-beds, these are the important things. And freedom from enemies, too. So as a fisherman works his way upstream at the end of the season, he will probably cast a critical eye over his water, his mind busy with plans. Those shallows above the wood, for instance—the trout will be spawning there soon. If they were raked, and the gravel loosened, the trout-eggs would have a better chance of safe cover between the stones. Here is one job to be done without delay. Then how about those other shallows, where there is even less depth of water, where the stream rushes and bubbles and gurgles so hastily that few trout can lie there without having to fight the current? Can anything be done? A few boulders, scattered over the shallows, would at least provide shelter for one or two trout and insects. Or better still, a dam or groyne just downstream would raise the level of the water a few inches, hold it up, slow it down, allow weed to grow and trout to live above the obstruction.

Perhaps, again, the fisherman may pass by a slow, silted stretch of water, half-choked by weed, some of it dying. He has caught very few fish in it this season. One or two trout do live there, but they do not rise and—yes, he can see a pike basking on the top of the water by the reeds. What should be done? The pike, of course, can be wired or electrocuted. If there are plenty of pike, they may even provide some good sport on rod and line during the winter.

But this is not getting to the root of the problem. The real trouble is that the current is too sluggish. It is not fast enough to carry particles of silt along so it deposits them. Even if all the mud were scooped out—which can be arranged, at some expense—exactly the same thing would happen later. The current would deposit more silt, clumps of still-water weed would begin to grow again, and the pike would re-establish themselves. No—either the amount of water must be increased, so that it flows faster, or the area over which it flows must be made smaller. The only way of obtaining more water, unfortunately, is to take it from somewhere else. Sometimes this is a practical possibility, when the river has a system of hatches leading to side-streams or carriers, but often it can be dangerous, since other parts of the river may suffer, or the whole irrigation system of the meadows be upset.

The second measure, however, is often feasible. It means, in effect, narrowing the river-bed. If hurdles, for instance, are staked into the river, jutting diagonally out from the bank, the current will flow faster as it goes round the hurdles. If each hurdle has a similar one opposite it on the far bank, the current will then be concentrated in the centre of the stream and will sweep the mud away. Silt will only be deposited in limited areas, in the slow water behind the hurdles. These deposits can be planted with sedges, and later with other vegetation, so that they become firm. Eventually the hurdles can be moved to do their work elsewhere, leaving behind them a stretch of water with a faster flow and a cleaner river-bed in the middle. Alternatively hurdle islands can be built in mid-stream, with the object of diverting and concentrating the flow on either side. Used properly, the current is by far the cheapest and best means of keeping the river free from too much silt.

Then, the fisherman will inspect his weeds closely—almost as lovingly as a gardener inspecting his flower-beds. Will there be enough water-plants next year to provide cover for trout and food for trout-food? He wants clean weed, growing on gravel if possible. Surveying the river bed, he can see plenty of starwort, with its starry clusters of tiny leaves. Ranunculus and water-celery are plainly in evidence, too. All these are good weeds, holding plenty of fly and shrimp. But there are some bad weeds about as well—mare's tail and long, wavy ribbon-weed. These are not nearly so hospitable to trout-food.

Should he try to root these bad weeds out? Perhaps so, if there are many of them. Mere cutting will be no long-term remedy. But if he uproots them, he may well be able to encourage more useful weeds to grow in their place, weeds that collect algae but not mud, weeds that will harbour thriving colonies of fly-larvae. Of these the starwort is probably the most adaptable. It will grow in quite fast water, and also in slow water. Its main trouble is that it does tend to collect silt. Where the current is fast enough to keep it clean and well oxygenated, it is a useful weed and will provide a home for many of the creatures that trout feed on. But where the current is slow—and particularly where it is slow and shallow—it will quickly become clogged with silt and may soon begin to choke the stream. A useful rule-of-thumb is to try to eliminate starwort where the water is less than eighteen inches deep, but to leave a fair growth of it elsewhere.

Rather better than the starwort are two weeds called ranunculus (or water buttercup) and water-celery. Small water-animals live in them readily, and they collect comparatively little silt. These weeds will not flourish in very deep or very sluggish water, but they grow well in most stretches of the chalk streams. Usually, if other weeds are removed to make room for them, they will take root naturally. Or you can plant them by dropping them into the river with stones tied to their roots, heavy enough to keep them in place while they gain a hold on the river bed. Or bunches of them, with their roots tied up in hessian bags, can be pushed into the silt or into holes dug in the gravel.

We all dream of perfect trout water. We shall love and cherish it, and we shall have the freedom of it. If it is a lake or reservoir, we may perhaps dream of beating the trout record every year. We can imagine ourselves, in a decade or two, feeling rather sorry for the members of the British Record (Rod-Caught) Fish Committee. Every year they will have to mutter into their grey beards: 'Not Mr . . . *again!*'

If we enjoy rivers more, we may not be able to dream up visions of such large fish. But to compensate for this, our dreams will be in colour, the bright colours of green and gold. There will be the vivid green of healthy weed and the gold of clean gravel. The trout will be many, and fat, and free-rising, because the stream will be full of food for them. Our perfect water will be a paradise for trout and for ourselves.

We all carry these dreams in our minds, and we hug them to our hearts. The tragedy is that although we could often do so much towards bringing them to life on our own rivers, we seldom do quite enough. Frequently we try to have our cake and eat it. We catch trout, and still expect to find them there next week. Sometimes we fail to take proper care not to fish for undersized fish. Sometimes, during the Mayfly or on other duffers' days, we keep more fish than we have any right to expect. Again, when we realise perfectly well that a day or two spent with stakes and hurdles and spades, instead of fishing rods, would repay us amply—we prefer to fish on.

But no-one can stop us dreaming. And as we walk up the riverbank in September, we rehearse all the thoughts and hopes that will support us through the coming close-season. We shall see those green banks from arm-chairs, from bus-queues and from office desks.

Meanwhile, however, the last evening of the last day has arrived, and we are fishing the evening rise for the very last time. There has been plenty of fly, and we have done well, but now it is almost too dark to fish at all. One trout is still rising. He has refused us frequently already. Perhaps one last cast would catch him? No? Then, one more. No? Just a final one, then. No. A flight of ducks whistles overhead, and a breath of cold air rustles the reed-tops.

It is September 30th. The season is over.

——◆◆◆◆ PART FOUR ◆◆◆◆——

Odds and Ends

CHAPTER 13

The Most Suitable Flyfishing Tackle

The title of this chapter has been advisedly chosen. It is far more important to obtain suitable flyfishing tackle than expensive tackle. Your tackle must be right for the sort of flyfishing you want to do, which need by no means involve you in spending a fortune.

How do you set about getting the right tackle? First, remember that no rod can be best at everything. (The most suitable rod for distance-casting on reservoirs will not, for instance, be suitable for delicate flyfishing on small streams.) You will have to make some choices between different sorts of tackle.

Distance or Delicacy

This is probably the most important choice of all. Will you need to cast a long way, even if it means sacrificing presentation (i.e. putting a fly down very accurately, very gently, very delicately)? Or will it be wiser to concentrate on better presentation at shorter distances? The decision will depend to a large extent on the waters you will be fishing and how they will be fished. Fishing from the shores of large still waters such as reservoirs will almost certainly require equipment that enables long-distance casting. It is virtually essential. But fishing overgrown little brooks, to take the opposite extreme, requires accuracy and delicacy, not distance. A long and powerful rod would only be an encumbrance. Between these two extremes are many other types of water, such as small lakes or ponds, and large or medium-size rivers. Each of these requires tackle which provides the right balance between distance and presentation.

All these considerations will be discussed later on. But meanwhile, try to imagine the sort of water you are most likely to fish. It will help to avoid making basic mistakes in the choice of tackle. If you expect to fish several different sorts of water you can always choose 'compromise' tackle—but then you can at least make sure that it is not unsuitable for the waters you will probably be fishing most frequently.

An Explanation

As you read the next few pages you may wonder why they deal with wet-fly tackle and salmon tackle and sea-trout tackle as well as with dry-fly tackle. One reason for this is that it is extremely useful to be able to compare the various types and to realise exactly how and why they differ from each other. Then another and perhaps more practical reason is that you are really most unlikely to confine yourself to the dry fly for all your flyfishing. So the information here about other sorts of flyfishing tackle may, I hope, be welcome and helpful.

How Good 'Balance' Assists Casting

The phrase 'balanced tackle' is often heard. What does it mean? 'Balanced tackle' means well-matched tackle—i.e. a set of tackle in which each individual item is well suited to the others. The two items which *must* suit each other are the rod and line.

A rod works in much the same way as an archer's bow—which has to bend before it can shoot an arrow. Similarly, a rod has to flex backwards before it can propel a line forwards. A rod can also be compared with a springboard—which has to be 'loaded' before it can store up or release energy. When casting, the rod is flexed by the weight of the line in the air pulling at the rod-tip. It isn't the angler who flexes the rod, the weight of the line is responsible for that.

Rods vary in flexibility. Flylines vary in weight. The weight of the flyline must be just right for the flexibility of the rod. If the flyline is too light, the rod will be underloaded. It will not flex as it should and it will not propel the line. If the line is too heavy, the rod will be overloaded and will not be able to keep the line moving properly through the air. If the line is much too heavy it may even strain or break the rod. If on the other hand the weight of the flyline matches the rod correctly, the advantages are two-fold:

(*a*) The rod will flex properly and will send the line out straight and true.

(*b*) Casting will soon become a pleasure, as it should be, and will never seem like hard work.

So the partnership of rod and line is absolutely vital. Other aspects of 'balanced tackle' are less important.

The Flyline—First and Foremost

The whole purpose of the rod is to propel the flyline. Neither rod nor reel can therefore be wisely chosen until the type and weight of the flyline have been settled. Everything starts with the line—and in particular with its weight.

The Importance of Weight

Unlike spinning lines or coarse-fishing lines, flylines are purposely made to have weight so that they can bend a flyrod. The various weights of line are classified according to AFTM numbers. (AFTM stands for Association of Fishing Tackle Manufacturers, which devised the classification.) The various numbers denote the relative weights of the first 30 ft of flyline—plus any level tip. The AFTM scale goes from 1 to 12, each successive number indicating a heavier line. The phrase 'AFTM No.' is usually shown as the symbol #. So if you see #6 on a flyline-box the line inside will be an AFTM No. 6 line.

Light lines (#2 to #5) can only be used with a flexible rod that is neither stiff nor very powerful. Used with such rods, light lines have certain advantages. They land gently on the water and are not likely to frighten the fish by making a splash. They cast less shadow, because they are thinner than heavier lines. Thus they are excellent for difficult conditions such as clear, calm, low water or bright sunshine. And they are particularly useful for shy trout.

Light lines can and should be used whenever you don't have to cast a long way or into a strong wind. They are ideal on small streams or medium-sized rivers like the Hampshire chalk streams. They are occasionally useful on still waters as well—for instance, when fishing calm water near the shore, or fishing downwind from a boat.

Heavy lines (#8 to #10) can and should be used with a stiff-ish and more powerful rod. (A less powerful rod would not be able to handle the weight of the line.) Heavy lines have advantages which are quite different from those of light lines. Their weight adds to their momentum when casting, helping them to travel a long way and to overcome air- and wind-resistance. Heavy lines are therefore preferable to light lines whenever distance is more important than perfect presentation. (In a particularly tricky wind, it is also a good idea to use a line one size heavier than usual.) For instance, on large still waters heavy lines or fairly heavy lines are advisable. Here the *capacity* to cast a long way is essential, even though it may be possible to catch plenty of fish at shorter range as well. Perfect presentation (especially when there's a ripple or wave on the water) is less vital. Even with a heavy-ish line, however, presentation can with practice be fairly good. #11 and #12 lines are for big salmon rods.

Medium-weight lines (#6 and #7) are the workaday general-purpose lines used by most fishermen. They cast farther than light-weight lines and perform a little better in a wind, though they will not touch down on the water so lightly or delicately. Neverthless, they present a fly perfectly well enough in most circumstances. A #6 line, for instance, is the weight most commonly used for dry-fly fishing on rivers, where considerable delicacy is needed.

Although medium-weight lines are less easy than heavier lines to cast a long way, they will achieve sufficient distance for almost any river, and for small still waters as well. Because of the superior presentation they allow, they are better than heavy lines for ponds and small lakes—though heavier lines are needed on big reservoirs. Used with rods of average flexibility they are ideal for all-purpose flyfishing—with the single exception of reservoirs and large still waters.

Floating or Sinking?

During recent decades great advances have been made in the design and manufacture of flylines. Each line usually consists of a core surrounded by a plastic 'dressing' and it is the density of the latter (i.e. whether it's denser or less dense than water) which determines whether a line floats or sinks. Furthermore, different sinking lines can have dressings of different densities which lead them to sink at differing speeds. Thus there are 'extra-fast-sinking lines' (with the most dense dressing), 'fast-sinking lines' and 'slow-sinking lines'. The denser the dressing of a flyline of a given weight, the thinner it will be. Four different #6 lines, for instance, would have identical weights but they would have different diameters if they happened to be, say, floating, slow-sinking, fast-sinking and extra-fast-sinking lines. The floating line would be the thickest.

When should you use a floating line, and when a sinking line? Obviously, dry-fly fishing demands a floating line. Not quite so obviously, so does a great deal of wet-fly and nymph fishing. When a wet fly or nymph is used with a floating line, its weight draws some or all of the leader—the length of nylon between line-tip and fly—beneath the surface. The heavier the fly and the slower the current, the more nylon will be taken down—and the last foot or so of the line may also be drawn under. Theoretically, if you're fishing still water with a floating line and a fairly heavy wet fly or nymph, you can fish as deep as your leader is long. Normally, however, the process of retrieving the line tends to raise the fly closer to the surface. But even so, lengthening the leader is a good way of fishing a little deeper than usual.

Floating lines, then, should be used for fishing on or near the surface. Their uses include:

(*a*) All dry-fly fishing on both still and running water.
(*b*) Wet-fly fishing for trout on almost all rivers. Fish which are ready to take will be 'up in the water' and a floating line normally gets flies deep enough.
(*c*) Most wet-fly fishing for sea-trout, whether by day or night, in any kind of water. Some sea-trout are caught on sinking lines, but far fewer than are caught on floating lines.
(*d*) A great deal of flyfishing for salmon, particularly in summer when the water is comparatively warm. In early spring and autumn a sinking line will probably be better, since salmon take deep when the water is cold.
(*e*) Wet-fly or nymph fishing for stillwater trout with many of the 'imitative' (as opposed to 'attractor') patterns of fly. These are

often most effective when fished fairly close to the surface and retrieved very slowly.

A further advantage of a floating line is the ease with which it can be 'picked up' from the surface for re-casting. This makes it an excellent line for beginners. A sinking line needs more practice before it can be handled well. Sinking lines are, however, essential as an alternative on nearly all still waters. Many stillwater fishermen catch more trout on them than on floating lines. They are virtually obligatory for the following purposes:

(*a*) Fast, deep retrieving in still water. This is often carried out with large wet flies called 'lures', and for these a fast-sinking or extra-fast sinking line is usually vital.

(*b*) Fishing really deep in still water even when retrieving *slowly*. Again a fast-sinking or extra-fast-sinking line will be necessary—because even these take far longer to reach the depths than most people imagine.

(*c*) Fishing fairly close to the surface in still water—whenever you're retrieving at a speed faster than 'very slow'. (A floating line, unless retrieved *very* slowly, brings the fly to the surface.) In these conditions a *slow-sinking* line is often best.

(*d*) Flyfishing for salmon when the water is 'heavy' and cold. Then a fast-sinking line and a comparatively large, weighty fly will usually be called for.

One other type of line should be mentioned. It is called a 'sink-tip' line—and is in fact a floating line except for its tip, which consists of several yards of sinking line. It is not one of the most commonly used lines, but it can be very handy in certain circumstances:

(*a*) Salmon fishermen find it useful whenever and wherever the current might make a fly skate along the surface if fished on a floating line—e.g. in the glide at the tail of a pool. Then a sink-tip line keeps the fly swimming where it should be—just below the surface.

(*b*) Stillwater trout fishermen (and a few wet-fly river fishermen) occasionally use it too—when they need a line that fishes a fly slightly deeper than a floating line but not so deep as a sinking line.

Fishing a still water from a drifting boat with a wet fly, or a team of wet flies, is usually practised with a floating line. If the boat is anchored, however, the same range of lines can be used as from the shore.

Many river fishermen never need any line other than a floating line. But a stillwater fisherman needs to be able to vary the depth at which he fishes—and also the speed at which he retrieves. One floating line and one sinking line, at the very least, should accompany him on his fishing trips. Serious and successful stillwater fishermen often carry more lines—3, 4 or even 5—to suit different conditions and different fishing techniques. They would feel unbearably handicapped if they did not allow themselves this degree of versatility. Their choice of line will frequently be more important to them than their choice of rod.

Which Sort of Taper?

All good flylines taper. They are designed so that there is a comparatively thick part near the tip-ring of the rod which helps in providing weight to flex the rod itself. They then taper down to a fine tip at the end of the line—which allows for delicacy and a smooth transmission of impetus from rod-tip to line-tip. Level or untapered lines, which can still be obtained, cannot perform nearly so well.

There are four main varieties of taper—double-taper, forward-taper (also called weight-forward), shooting head, and finally single-taper (often called a half-line). The first two of these are 'full lines'— usually 30 yards long, sometimes 40 yards for salmon. The standard shooting head is only 10 yards in length, while a single-taper line is a 'half-line' and is therefore normally 15 yards long. The profiles of these various tapers are shown diagrammatically on page 142.

Each taper behaves in a different way and has a different purpose. One of the main differences lies in the amount of line you can 'shoot' (*see* p. 19). The extra distance gained by shooting depends largely on the taper of the line.

Double-taper lines are the most popular type. They have several advantages and only one disadvantage:

(*a*) Since the two halves of a double-taper line are identical, it has two usable ends. When one end begins to wear out, you can simply reverse the line on the reel and use the other end. Thus each line has a double life.

(b) They are easy to cast, because however much line is aerialised there is always thick line at the rod-tip. (This is important for good casting and less easy to judge with a forward-taper line—see below.) For the same reason, a double-taper line turns over smoothly in the air—and this helps good presentation. Double-taper lines are by far the best for beginners.

(c) So far, so good. But double-taper lines are not particularly efficient for really long-distance casting, because the friction of the thick line in the rod-rings will prevent you shooting it a very long way.

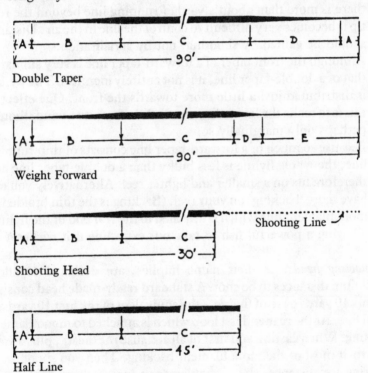

Double Taper

Weight Forward

Shooting Line

Shooting Head

Half Line

LINE TAPERS. *A* = LEVEL LINE-TIP: *2 ft long. B* = FRONT TAPER: *8–10 ft. C* = belly: *65–70 ft for double lines, 14–30 ft for forward-taper lines, according to 'lift' required. D* = REAR TAPER: *same as front taper for double-taper lines, 3–8 ft for forward lines. E* = RUNNING LINE: *used only for 'shooting'*

Forward-taper or weight-forward lines are fairly similar to double-taper lines so far as the part that you aerialise is concerned—i.e. the first dozen yards or so. But then, instead of a long thick 'belly' and a reverse taper at the other end, the rest of a forward-taper line consists of thin 'running line' (*see* page 142). Here are the characteristics of forward-taper lines:

(*a*) You can with practice shoot a good deal more of a forward-taper line than of a double-taper line, because the thin running line slips more easily through the rod-rings than the thicker belly of the double-taper. Greater distance is therefore possible. But too much forward-taper line should never be aerialised—because if there is more than about a yard of running line beyond the rod-tip it becomes very difficult to control the line in the air. Distance should be gained by shooting, not by aerialisation.

(*b*) Although the front taper of a forward-taper line is very similar to that of a double-taper line, it is not entirely identical. The weight is distributed just a little more towards the front. One effect of this is to make the line turn over a little better into a wind, though perhaps only marginally so.

(*c*) Because so much of a forward-taper line consists of thin running line, the whole flyline is less bulky than a double-taper line and therefore fits on a smaller and lighter reel. Alternatively you can have more 'backing' on your reel. (Backing is the thin braided or monofilament line which is attached to the rear end of the flyline, allowing a powerful fish to take out extra line if it wishes.)

Shooting heads, as their name implies, are designed to allow maximum distances to be shot. A standard ready-made head consists of only 10 yards or so of flyline—the equivalent of the first 10 yards of a full line. At the rear end is a loop which is attached to monofilament backing. When casting you first of all aerialise the 'head', plus a yard or two at most of the monofilament backing. Then you shoot more backing for distance, the monofilament running through the rod-rings with even greater ease than the running line of a forward-taper line.

A shooting head needs a certain amount of practice to be handled well. The abrupt change in diameter from monofilament to flyline makes it more difficult to achieve smooth turn-over and good presentation. In addition, some fishermen prefer the feel of ordinary flyline to the feel of monofilament in their left hands. With these provisos, however, a shooting head is an extremely efficient type of line for distance-casting and is the favourite of many reservoir fishermen. Some salmon fishermen also use it in order to cover a wide river. It takes up even less room on a spool than does a forward-taper line, permitting a very small, light reel and ample backing.

The idea of the loop at the butt-end of a ready-made shooting head is to allow a quick change to a heavier or lighter head. Most fishermen, however, only use one head on any single reel or spare spool. A smoother join can then be made by cutting off the loop and needle-knotting (*see* next chapter) the monofilament to the rear end of the shooting head.

Single-taper lines—commonly called half-lines—are quite widely used these days. They consist of half a double-taper line and therefore only cost about half as much. Furthermore, they have certain advantages:

(*a*) They provide quite enough flyline for most purposes—45 ft of line plus 9 ft of leader, plus say 9 ft of rod, is ample for casts of about 20 yards.

(*b*) Half-lines are obviously less bulky than full lines, and allow small, light reels to be used.

(*c*) They can easily be made into home-made shooting heads. This is the type that many good flyfishermen prefer, since they may wish to aerialise rather more than the 10 yards of a standard head. Fifteen yards is usually too much, however, so they often snip off about three yards from the back of the half-line to leave themselves with a 12-yard shooting head, which they then needle-knot to monofilament backing.

If you make up a shooting head in this way, remember that the AFTM No. of any line is based on the weight of the first 30 ft (plus the level tip). If you aerialise more than 30 ft, you are in effect loading the rod with a higher AFTM No. As a rough guide, each extra 6 ft adds one AFTM No. A 12-yard shooting head made from #7 line will therefore weigh as much as a standard 10-yard #8 shooting head, and will be suitable for a rod that casts best with a #8 line.

12. ADVICE from good fishermen is always worth seeking and listening carefully to. Few can fail to benefit from the wisdom and acquired knowledge of others, especially if they happen to be as pre-eminent as the late Frank Sawyer. The photograph shows Dermot Wilson learning a great deal about nymphs and nymph-fishing from Frank Sawyer during a day's fishing on the Itchen. (*Renée Wilson*)

13. FERGUS WILSON, the author's son, acts as ghillie to the late Dick Walker. There is no better way for a boy to learn than by watching and helping experienced fishermen who are prepared to pass on their knowledge to him. Fergus Wilson is now a grown-up fisherman himself – but he remains grateful to the many people who gave him wise advice.

14. A TROUT being unhooked before release will recover all the sooner if he can be kept underwater during the process – as in this photograph. A barbless hook makes it easy to release a trout in this way. As Chapter 11 explains, surprisingly few fish are lost when a barbless hook is used – and in fact rather more fish are hooked instead of being merely 'pricked'.

15. A BADLY-HOOKED TROUT may have to be lifted gently from the water before being unhooked, so that the hook itself can be seen and gently eased out. One little-known fact is that if a trout is held upside-down, as in the photograph, he will normally struggle far less than if held back-uppermost. Hands should of course be thoroughly wettened first, to avoid removing too much of the protective slime that covers a trout's whole body. The trout in the picture appears to have a slightly distorted vent. This is not a wound but a minor malformation.

12

13

14

15

The Colour of Flylines

We cannot be sure what a flyline looks like to a fish. Underwater photographs have been taken—and observers have often sunk themselves below the surface to look up at flylines—but we can never take it for granted that a fish sees things as we do. Nevertheless, it is usually assumed that a flyline is least visible to a fish when it corresponds in tone (rather than colour) to the background against which it will be seen. Here are some guidelines:

(*a*) A floating line is often seen by fish against the background of the sky. It will therefore be least conspicuous if it is light in tone. White and light orange are two useful colours. In many circumstances, however, the colour of a floating line is not very important. A shy trout may be frightened by a line of any colour, so it is best not to let him see it at all. Apart from the fly, only the leader should be in his vision.

(*b*) On some waters, such as those bordered by tall trees, a floating line is more likely to be seen against foliage. Then a darker colour, such as green or brown, may be preferable.

(*c*) Sinking lines are normally seen against a dark background and are therefore fairly dark in tone—either green or brown.

(*d*) Despite the above, there does exist a minority body of opinion which believes a dark-coloured line to be the least obvious to trout in all situations, whether the line is a floating or sinking one. They may be right. No-one knows for certain. But even so, when a floating line is being chosen, the extra visibility of a light-coloured line to the fisherman is a balancing factor to take into account. It may well tip the balance in its favour, at any rate for those who find it useful to see their line clearly on the water—often very important when fishing a nymph.

Manufacturers' Markings

All flylines are described by a combination of letters and numbers which appear on the box and are used in catalogues. These markings are made up of three components which describe (1) the type of taper, (2) the AFTM No. and (3) the floating/sinking properties of the line. The abbreviations and the order in which they are used are shown below:

DT = double-taper
WF = weight-forward, i.e. forward
      taper
ST = shooting-taper, i.e. shooting
      head. Also, though rarely,
      single-taper

AFTM No.

F   = floating
S   = sinking
F/S = float/sink
      i.e. sink-tip
I   = intermediate

For example, a DT—6—F line is a #6 double-taper floating line, an ST—8—S line is a #8 shooting head made of sinking line and a WF—7—F/S is a #7 forward-taper sink-tip line. An intermediate line is one that will float when greased and sink just a little when ungreased.

Choosing a Trout Rod

As we have seen already, the weight of the flyline should dictate the flexibility of the rod. All modern flyrods have the weight of line for which they were designed marked on the butt just above the handle.

The Right Length

For convenience let us describe any rod longer than 9 ft as 'long', any rod from 8 to 9 ft as 'medium-length' and any rod under 8 ft as 'short'. All have their uses.

Long rods:
(a) They are at their most effective on reservoirs and other large still waters, where distance is usually more important than perfect presentation. They are also very useful for wet-fly fishing on large or fair-sized rivers.
(b) For distance-casting, they should be powerful enough to handle a fairly heavy line (at least #7 or #8) provided always that the rod is not so heavy or so stiff that it becomes tiring to use. These characteristics in turn depend to some extent on the material from which the rod is made (*see* p. 148). For instance, any single-handed cane rod longer than 9 ft is liable to tire the average fisherman. Fibreglass is considerably lighter—a 9¼ ft or 9½ ft glass rod weighing about 5 oz can be first-class for still water. Some stillwater fishermen can even use a 10 ft glass rod. Carbon fibre is the lightest rod-making material of all—a 9½ or 10 ft rod

can weigh 4 oz and be easy to handle all day. Even longer carbon-fibre rods are perfectly practicable—but weight isn't everything. The extra leverage exerted on the wrist by a very long rod should also be borne in mind.

(c) A long rod—10 ft or longer—is useful when 'drift fishing' from a boat with a 'team' of wet flies. Trout often take the 'top dropper' (the fly nearest the rod-tip) as you retrieve it and bring it skipping along the surface of the water. Since this is done by raising the rod-tip, a rod with a good deal of length is always helpful.

A *medium-length rod* (8 to 9 ft) is an ideal all-purpose rod for smaller still waters and for nearly all rivers other than little brooks and streams. Here are some comments:

(a) A 9 ft rod is a very good all-rounder, capable of adequate distance for large still waters and perfect for smaller still waters. Furthermore, it is not too long or cumbersome for most rivers. A 9 ft single-handed cane rod may be a little on the heavy side, but not for those who particularly like cane. A 9 ft fibreglass or carbon-fibre rod will be light enough for anyone except perhaps a child.

(b) Rods from 8 to 8¾ ft are primarily river-fishing rods and are perfect for the dry fly. Whichever material they're made of, they are light enough to handle easily and will present a fly exceptionally well. A river fisherman should choose a rod-length which suits the size of stream he fishes—8 to 8½ ft is long enough for most medium-sized streams. Remember, presentation is more important than distance on almost any river—at any rate with a dry fly. If you are consistently fishing the wet fly on a river, however, good presentation will be less vital and you can use a longer rod if you wish. By holding the rod at 45°, as you should, you can use the extra length to lift the belly of the line more easily over awkward currents, while the angle of the rod will make it more sensitive to any sudden take from a trout.

(c) 8½ ft is a good length for any young flyfisher from about the age of 7. If it is made of fibreglass, for instance, it will be quite light enough for him or her and can cost very little. It is a mistake to give a youngster a 'miniature' rod of under 8 ft because he will find it all the more difficult to keep his backcast well up behind him. Remember that he is closer to the ground than an adult anyway.

A *short flyrod* (under 8 ft and occasionally no more than 6 ft) is extremely useful for brook fishing. Also, it can give great pleasure to anyone fishing a wider stream who enjoys using a small, delicate rod with as light a line as possible. Like other lengths of rod, it has its own advantages and one or two disadvantages:

(a) On a very overgrown little brook a short rod allows you to cast in and among bushes and trees.

(b) Even if it's made of cane (the heaviest rod-making material) it will still be very light and very pleasant to use.

(c) Although short rods can be made stiff enough to throw fairly heavy lines, they are also ideal for light lines (#4, or even #3) and thus for very delicate fishing.

(d) Short rods need practice to handle well because there is 'less rod' to do the work. They also make it a little harder to keep the backcast up in the air. Beginners are therefore wise to start with a rod of 8 ft or longer.

(e) When playing a fish, you have less control with a short rod than with a longer one. For instance, it is less easy to keep a trout away from weeds.

Which Material for a Trout Rod?

So far I have spoken of cane and fibreglass and carbon-fibre rods almost as if they were equally popular. This is a long way from being the real situation. Infinitely the most popular material today, well in front of the others, is carbon fibre—or carbon fibre mixed either with boron or, less frequently, Kevlar. Nearly all so called 'boron' rods are in fact a mix of the two substances, and the same applies to Kevlar rods. For convenience I shall refer to them all from now on as 'carbon fibre', since their properties differ hardly at all.

Cane rods are used by only a very small minority of flyfishermen these days. But the minority happens to be an extremely devoted one, since cane continues to have certain pleasant and useful characteristics which no other material possesses. When fibreglass first appeared shortly after the World War II, every prophet of doom predicted the early demise of cane. When carbon fibre arrived the very same predictions were made. Yet cane rods remained on the scene and will probably continue to do so—however much in the minority—for untold years ahead.

Fibreglass rods, from the time of their invention to the time when carbon fibre set the flyfishing world by the ears, were the most popular rods of the day, far more popular than cane. But now you hardly ever see them being advertised and many manufacturers have given up making them. This seems a pity, since fibreglass makes it possible to produce an extremely serviceable rod which costs very little indeed. Nevertheless, happily enough, fibreglass rods are still available. Hardy's, to quote just one instance, still make them. And so do a few other manufacturers. Thank goodness for that.

Since all three materials are still on the market, it seems only sensible to comment on each of them.

A Preliminary Comment

There is no material in the world which by itself can guarantee you a good rod. Excellent rods, for their individual purposes, are made from all three materials—but so also are some appallingly bad rods. The design of the rod—which dictates the way in which it casts—can be just as important as the material from which it has been constructed.

This makes it very wise to try a rod out before you buy it. Then you can satisfy yourself that it suits both you and the purpose for which you intend to use it. Unfortunately, simply waggling a rod in a shop gives you absolutely no idea of how it will perform. You have to cast with it yourself, not only with the right weight of line but with a leader and fly as well. Trying it with the line alone may well give you a false impression.

Many of the best tackle shops, other than in London, now have facilities which enable you to try out rods. Go to one of them, even if it costs a little to get there. If this proves impossible, or if you decide to buy your rod by mail-order, then see if you can find a friend who already possesses the rod you have in mind, and ask him if you can have a cast with it. Buying a rod you have never handled is to invite disappointment.

Speed of Action

You will see that rods of certain materials are described below as being 'fast' or 'slow'. This refers to the speed with which they are capable of bending and unbending—quite often called the 'rate of recovery'. A rod with a 'fast' rate of recovery tends to throw a comparatively 'narrow loop' as shown on p. 154. A rod with a slow rate of recovery tends to throw a fairly 'wide loop', as on p. 154. (The word 'tend' has been used because the skill of the caster can also affect the width of the loop.)

A narrow loop, because it obviously offers less air-resistance, is a considerable help if you are trying to cast a long distance and also when you are casting into a strong wind. On the other hand a wide loop, because it turns over in a more unhurried way, makes it easier to put a fly delicately on the water. It can also assist accuracy, except in high winds.

And now for the characteristics of the three materials.

Carbon Fibre (called graphite in the USA)

The most immediately noticeable feature of all carbon-fibre rods is their lightness. A typical 8½ ft dry-fly rod, for instance, can weigh as little as 3 oz or less—depending to some extent on the weight of the rod-fittings, i.e. the reel-mount, rod-rings, etc.

As the length of the rod increases, the extra lightness of carbon fibre, compared with any other material, becomes even more important. It means that young people, for the first time, can handle reasonably long and powerful stillwater rods—such as a 9½ ft rod weighing well under 4 oz, yet easily able to cast a #7 or #8 line. Adults also can of course use longer-than-ever rods without any strain at all, whenever they find it useful. There is, for instance, a singlehanded 11¼ ft rod which is ideal for drift-fishing on stillwater. It weighs only 4 oz and can carry a light line.

So far as speed of action is concerned, a carbon-fibre rod can now be made to have any action required of it. In this sense it is again unique. You can have either a 'fast' rod for long-distance or into-the-wind casting or a 'slow' rod for extremely delicate presentation with a very light line. Or anything in-between. The in-between actions, avoiding either extreme, are in fact, not unnaturally, the best for any rod that has to operate in a variety of different conditions and situations.

Yet another unique property of carbon-fibre rods is their 'tolerance' for different line weights. Most will cast very adequately indeed with three weights of line, or perhaps even more, though you may find just one of them to be ideal. A good 8½ ft carbon-fibre dry-fly rod, for example, is likely to be able to handle a #4 line or a #5 line or a #6 line. You may normally use the #5 as the ideal, but still think it worth carrying the other two weights on spare spools for your reel. The #4 may prove very useful for ultra-delicate presentation on calm water and in calm weather, while the heavier #6 will come into its own if you have to cast into a strong wind.

As regards cost, the earliest carbon-fibre rods were extremely high-priced, since all the 'rod-blanks' came from America. But now they are being made in a great many other places, including countries where labour is not at all expensive, so that you can obtain carbon-fibre rods today which are very affordable indeed, costing less than cane rods and not a great deal more than fibreglass rods. The best-reputed rods, however, are made either in this country or in America and are still comparatively dear, more so than a good cane rod. If you decide to buy one of the lower-priced carbon-fibre rods, remember that while some of them are indeed very good, some are not. This makes it all the more important to try out as many rods as possible before arriving at a choice.

Cane (called bamboo in the USA)

In at least one way cane is the opposite of carbon fibre, since it is by far the heaviest of the three materials. This limits its usefulness considerably. A 9½ ft cane stillwater rod, for instance, would weigh at least 6½ oz, almost twice as much as an equivalent carbon-fibre rod, and would indeed be very tiring to use for any length of time. So cane rods can really be ruled out for stillwater fishing (except perhaps on small lakes and ponds) or—to my mind—for any sort of trout fishing that requires a rod of 9 ft or longer.

But when it comes to river fishing, the picture does change. A cane rod of under 9 ft can be used by most fishermen all day without any undue effort. (Fisherwomen and fisheryoungsters may prefer to set the limit at 8½ ft.) A cane brook rod of 6½ ft can weigh only 2½ oz and a 7½ ft rod under 4 oz. An 8 ft rod may weigh 4½ oz, an 8½ ft rod 4¾ oz, and an 8¾ ft rod a fraction over 5 oz. None of these could be described as a 'heavy rod'.

Cane also makes a very efficient river-fishing rod, especially for the dry fly. A cane dry-fly rod has a characteristic and fairly leisurely action which delivers a dry fly both gently and accurately. I myself like using a cane dry-fly rod just as much as a carbon-fibre dry-fly rod, and perhaps rather more. Yet it must be confessed that carbon-fibre rods can simulate the action of cane rods, and of course be a good deal lighter.

To compensate for this, however, people who enjoy using cane find that it gives them a great deal of psychological pleasure— something not to be dismissed lightly. They relish the idea and 'feel' of cane as the only truly 'natural' material among the three, the others being entirely man-made. In addition a cane rod is never mass-produced in the same way as carbon-fibre or fibreglass rods. Every cane rod, even if machines are used in its making (not always the case), receives far more individual attention from a craftsman. For these reasons it is far easier to develop a genuine and lasting affection for a cane rod than for a rod of any other material.

The cost of a good cane rod is usually in the middle of the carbon-fibre range. That is to say, it will be cheaper than the more expensive carbon-fibre rods but will cost more than very low-priced carbon-fibre rods. Cane, incidentally, does have one other unique feature, in that you can ask a master rod-builder to make you a completely individual cane rod, precisely the rod you want, entirely by hand. (Not possible with carbon-fibre or fibreglass.) Rods like this cost several hundred pounds, but their owners love them to distraction.

Fibreglass

So far as weight is concerned, fibreglass takes its place between cane and carbon fibre. An 8½ ft dry-fly rod may weigh about 3¾ oz, and a 9½ ft reservoir rod about 5 oz. It is therefore perfectly suitable for stillwater rods as well as river-fishing rods.

In fact fibreglass is usually at its best on stillwaters. This is because it has a typical action which is on the fast side, and so not at all bad for distance casting with fairly heavy lines. But the fast-ish action, combined with a certain lack of 'yield', does also lead to some drawbacks.

The chief disadvantage of fibreglass is probably the fact that it needs a good deal of 'pull' at the rod-tip before it starts flexing. This makes it less efficient than the other two materials for short-distance casting, with very little line out. It also means that fibreglass rods are incompatible with very light lines. An 8 ft or 8½ ft rod, for instance, will not be able to handle a line any lighter than a #6. Whilst this is not really too heavy for most river work, many dry-fly fishermen (including myself) prefer to use, say, a #5 for extra delicacy.

Fibreglass is therefore rather less efficient and far less versatile than carbon fibre. But rods made of it can be quite good enough to give excellent service. And it does have one very practical asset—its extremely low cost. It is less expensive than either cane or carbon fibre. This not only brings a fibreglass rod within the reach of almost anyone, but also allows people fishing on a low budget to have more than one rod if they wish. Someone who fishes both stillwaters and small streams, for instance, may be well advised to buy two fibreglass rods instead of (and for the same price as) a single so called 'all purpose' carbon-fibre rod.

Diameter

The comparative thickness of a rod may not be a major factor in its performance, but is well worth mentioning. The thinner a rod is, the less air resistance it will offer as you cast with it. This gives a slim rod some slight advantage (though hardly a critical advantage) over a thicker rod so far as distance casting is concerned—since it will not be slowed up by the air to the same extent. There is also the fact that many fishermen favour fairly slim rods on purely aesthetic grounds. As regards the three materials, fibreglass rods have the thickest diameters, followed by cane rods, followed in turn by carbon-fibre rods. Carbon-fibre rods are the slimmest.

Salmon and Sea-trout Rods

Flyrods for salmon are naturally more powerful than trout rods. Most of them are considerably longer too, and therefore designed for double-handed casting. The extra length of a salmon rod is not mainly for the handling of heavy fish, but to allow the fly to be fished

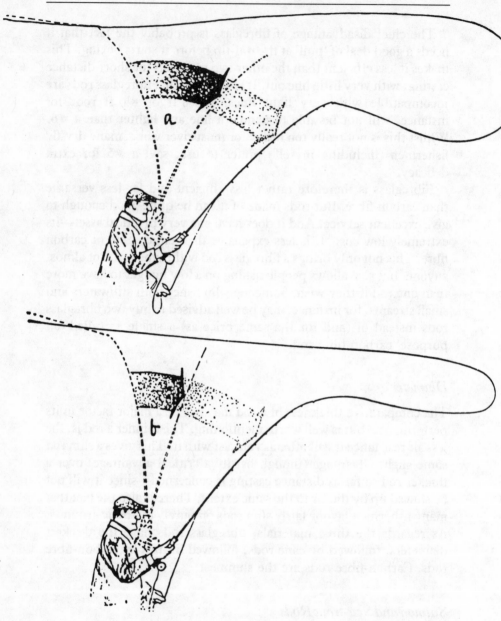

A rod with a 'slow' action (a, above) will tend to throw a 'wide loop', whereas a rod with a 'fast' action (b) will need to throw a 'narrow loop'. A narrow loop is better for distance-casting and the overcoming of wind-resistance. A wide loop helps delicate presentation.

more effectively. By enabling the line to be held out over tricky currents it helps the fisherman to let the fly swim exactly where he wishes (and at the right speed). Also, of course, it assists distance-casting on broad rivers.

Because of the length of the most desirable double-handed rods for salmon fishing, the lightest material of all—carbon fibre—is fast becoming almost universally used. Some cane rods still linger on, but when they are replaced a carbon-fibre rod is nearly always bought instead.

Carbon fibre has probably, in fact, been of even more value in salmon fishing than in trout fishing. It has meant that fairly young fisherpeople, as well as many fisherladies, can now use longer and therefore more efficient rods than they were ever able to handle before. (As a tribute to fisherladies, however, it should not be forgotten that for a long time some of them have been catching enviable numbers of salmon on more old-fashioned rods.) Adult salmon fishermen can now if they wish buy a rod as long as 20 ft which will not fatigue them. Before the arrival of carbon fibre, a rod of this length would have been quite impractical.

Double-handed carbon-fibre salmon rods are admittedly not inexpensive. But they are well worth trying to afford. If this proves impossible, have a look at such fibreglass salmon rods as you can find. They will be considerably cheaper than either carbon-fibre or cane rods, and quite light enough to allow you to use a rod of respectable length.

The exact length and power of the most suitable double-handed salmon rod or rods for your own fishing will depend on the size of the rivers to be visited—and also on the size of flies to be cast. The colder and 'heavier' the water, the larger the fly you will normally use. This is important. If you try to cast a large heavy fly such as a big brass tube-fly on a rod which is simply not powerful enough, you are very likely to hook yourself more often than you hook salmon. With only a little bad luck, you may well put a hook in your eye. This is why rods of the same length are often made in two versions—powerful and not-so-powerful.

Assuming that you are using carbon fibre, a fairly long and powerful rod of 16 or 17 ft is more suitable for big rivers and heavy coldwater flies. A far smaller rod of 12 or 13 ft can be excellent for narrow rivers and light summer flies. A rather more powerful rod is advisable for a sinking line than for a floating line, since more strain is put on the rod each time the line is retrieved from beneath the surface for recasting. A rod of about 15 ft, capable of handling a #9 line, makes a good all-round double-handed salmon rod. Smaller salmon rods will handle #8 lines, while larger ones may need lines up to #11 or #12.

Single-handed rods (from 9 to 10 ft) are also perfectly suitable on many rivers in summer conditions, when fairly light flies are being used. They are excellent for drift fishing on lochs as well. Such a rod should usually handle a #7 or #8 line.

A suitable rod for sea-trout need not be very different from an ordinary trout rod. Often the same rod will serve both purposes. A medium-length trout rod can be excellent for average-sized sea-trout in fairly small rivers. For larger sea-trout in larger rivers (or for drift fishing) the ideal rod would perhaps be 9 or 10 ft, designed for a #7 line. But a good reservoir rod makes a serviceable alternative and can often be used for light salmon as well.

Choosing a Flyreel

The choice of flyreel is a less vital matter than the choice of rod and line. Provided the reel is not altogether too heavy, it will have very little influence on casting performance. The main task of a flyreel is to store the flyline and backing in a convenient way. Obviously it should be reliable—most modern flyreels are—but it need not be either elaborate or expensive. A simple flyreel, which turns the drum once for each turn of the handle, is usually quite suitable. There are two main types:

(a) The traditional type, in which the spool revolves inside the cage. An adjustable 'check' or 'drag' is desirable to allow you to vary the degree of pull needed before the reel gives out line. Set the drag according to the strength of your tackle and the size of fish you expect.

(b) The 'rim control' type, in which the spool has a flange which revolves on the outside of the reel. This allows a running fish to be braked by lightly touching the rim as it turns round. An adjustable check can then be dispensed with, though it is often included as a useful extra.

Then there are two types of less simple reel:

(a) The multiplying reel has a gearing system which leads the drum to revolve more than once with each turn of the handle. The precise ratio varies with different reels but is normally in the region of 2-to-1.

(b) The automatic flyreel has a mechanism (usually clockwork) which does away with the necessity for any reel-handle at all. When a lever is depressed, the drum revolves automatically and winds line back onto the reel. Automatic reels, however are hardly ever seen these days—so I shall not mention them any further. ·

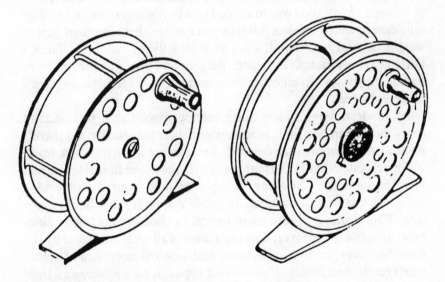

The traditional type of reel (left) and the 'rim control' type.

Multiplying reels have the distinct virtue of retrieving line far more rapidly than simple reels do. A good many fishermen find this a worthwhile and significant asset. Others, however, believe that a simple reel is easier and less stiff to turn than most multiplying reels. The choice is entirely a matter of personal preference. It's true that multiplying reels are just a little heavier than simple reels and also cost a little more. But they suit some fishermen very well indeed.

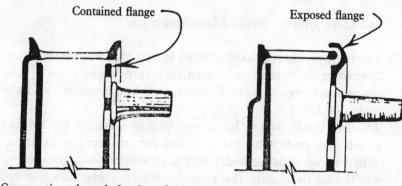

Contained flange

Exposed flange

Cross sections through the rims of the two principal kinds of flyreel (illustrated on p. 157)

It used to be said that the weight of a flyreel should 'balance the rod'. This is largely an old wives' tale, because there is no ideal 'point of balance'. Most rods would indeed cast best with no reel at all. The only case in which balance is important is when there is a good deal of weight beyond your hand, such as with a 9½ ft cane rod. Then a fairly heavy reel acts as a counter-balance and prevents the rod from feeling top-heavy. In all other circumstances, it is sensible to have a fairly light reel.

All modern flyreels have quick-release spools, so if you want to carry more than one line (as stillwater fishermen usually do) there's no need to have more than one reel. You can use spare spools instead.

There's one other important point to make about flyreels. The reel you choose must obviously be able to hold your flyline and a sufficient quantity of backing. In other words, it must be the right size. This makes it all the more logical to choose your line or lines before choosing your reel. The capacities of all reels are stated by the manufacturers in their catalogues and advertisements, and some-times on the reel boxes. These stated capacities are *sometimes* a little optimistic, so ask your tackle dealer to wind your line and backing onto the reel. Here are some other factors to bear in mind:

(*a*) A double-taper floating line requires more room than any other sort of line. For instance, if your reel holds a DT-6-F line with a given amount of backing, it will hold any other #6 flyline with more backing.

(*b*) Sinking lines take up less room than floating lines because they are thinner. Forward-taper lines take up less room than double-taper lines, and shooting heads or single-taper lines take up less room still.

(c) The required amount of backing depends on your type of fishing. On many rivers, especially small rivers, trout do not run far, so little or no backing is needed. Large open waters are a different matter, particularly if they hold large fish. At least 40 or 50 yards of backing will be necessary. And for salmon fishing on large waters you may well need 100 yards of backing.

(d) Make sure that the spool of the reel is 'bulked up' with sufficient backing so that the end of the flyline is about ¼" below the rim. If the spool is insufficiently filled, each revolution of the drum will take in very little line.

Leaders

Of all the items of tackle that a dry-fly fisherman uses, the leader or cast is perhaps the one that is most frequently neglected. Yet the composition and taper of a leader are vital to good casting and good presentation and therefore to good dry-fly fishing. In all circumstances which call for reasonable presentation, in fact, your leader should be just as carefully tapered as your flyline. Otherwise, however well you cast the flyline, your leader may fail to straighten out properly—especially against a wind. You are likely to find it falling in a sad and sorry little heap around your line-tip.

(Untapered leaders, however, consisting of a single length of level nylon, are perfectly adequate for most salmon and sea-trout fishing, since the current will anyway serve to straighten the leader. They can also be adequate for a good deal of wet-fly fishing for trout.)

Until not long ago all leaders were constructed wholly of solid monofilament, usually known simply as nylon. But in recent years an entirely new type of leader has appeared—with a butt made of 'braid'. This braid consists of many fine nylon strands braided together and usually accounts for rather more than half the total length of the leader. The two types of leader will be referred to below as ordinary nylon leaders and braided-butt leaders. Since the former type is at present more widely used than the latter (though the situation could easily be reversed before long) I will deal with it first.

The greater part of the information that follows, I should perhaps add, will be of most relevance to dry-fly fishermen, but some of it will affect other sorts of flyfishermen as well.

Ordinary nylon leaders

A frequent shortcoming of shop-bought dry-fly leaders (as opposed to home-made leaders) is that many of them have butts which are not thick enough. To continue the taper of the flyline into the leader, and to allow energy to flow without interruption from rod-tip to fly, the nylon at the leader-butt should have a diameter of at least 0.45 mm.

Another barrier to good presentation, though rather less important, is an over-bulky line-to-leader knot. The common figure-of-eight knot, for instance, is certainly on the bulky side. Learn to tie a needle-knot (*see* next chapter) if you can, because it makes the smoothest possible join between flyline and leader. Failing that, use one of the plastic cast connectors which are available in the shops.

The diameter of your leader-tip will probably be governed by several considerations. Large fish obviously warrant thicker and stronger leader-tips than small fish. Wary and 'well-educated' fish can often only be caught on comparatively fine leader-tips. Very bright weather or low, clear water may also call for a fine leader-tip. The size of fly is also important. A small fly behaves unnaturally if it's tied to a thick leader-tip. Equally, with a fine leader-tip it is difficult to turn over a large bushy fly such as a Mayfly against a contrary breeze. Leader-tips can be classified, perhaps rather arbitrarily, as shown in the table below. Very fine and fine leader-tips are suitable for river trout. So are medium leader-tips on occasion—when bigger than usual fish are expected, for instance, or when it is necessary to turn a big bushy fly over into a wind. Strong tips are useful for large reservoir fish and sea-trout, while extra-strong tips are for salmon.

Certain trout-diameters of nylon are often referred to (especially in America but also here) as 1X, 2X, 3X and so on. These designations, therefore, have been added to the actual measurements.

Leader-Tip Diameters (mm)

Very fine	0.12 (7×) and 0.14 (6×)
Fine	0.16 (5×) and 0.18 (4×)
Medium	0.20 (3×)
Strong	0.22 (2×) and 0.24 (1×)
Extra strong	0.28 to 0.35

It would be helpful, of course, if I could include breaking-strains in the table above. But the trouble is that different makes of nylon often have very different breaking strains. You may find, for instance, that the 0.18 mm diameter of one nylon will have a breaking-strain of 3¾ lb—but so will the 0.16 mm diameter of another nylon. This will also of course affect your choice of the best diameter to use.

(New nylons are constantly being produced these days with exceptionally high breaking-strains. Just one word of warning here. Some of them, however strong they may normally be, are a trifle brittle and have little 'shock-strength'. That is to say, they are not very good at withstanding a sudden strain. Others again have little 'knot strength' and can break with comparative ease at the knot which joins the leader-tip to the remainder of the leader. This is not to put you off new and improved nylons—for improvements are undoubtedly taking place. All in all, however, it is usually wiser to fish with a reasonably strong and utterly reliable nylon rather than with some stronger-than-ever-before nylon that lacks dependability.)

Confusingly enough, on spools of different nylons, the diameters of some are given in millimetres and some in inches. Here are the correct comparisons:

MM	IN	MM	IN
0.12	0.0047	0.22	0.0087
0.14	0.0055	0.24	0.0094
0.16	0.006	0.28	0.011
0.18	0.007	0.35	0.014
0.20	0.008		

Breaking-strains may be given either in lbs or kilos. But this is more simple. If you remember that 1 kilo amounts to just 2.2 lb, any necessary conversions hardly require a degree in higher mathematics.

Home-made leaders (the most economic) are made up by knotting together a number of lengths of nylon, stepping down the diameter at each knot. Here are some points to remember:

(a) Each step should reduce the diameter of the nylon by no more than 0.05 mm. Otherwise the leader will be liable to break at the knot. Use blood knots with no fewer than four turns on each side.

One other good knot for tying leaders is the water knot. It is very strong but rather bulky, and this makes it most suitable for joining *fine* lengths of nylon together.

(*b*) The first length of nylon, which forms the butt of the leader, should be a long one—almost half the total leader. This long, level butt helps the leader to turn over smoothly. Many good fishermen keep a 4 or 5 ft length of fairly thick nylon (0.45 or 0.50 mm) permanently needle-knotted to the tips of their fly-lines. When they wish to renew their leaders, they do so only from the end of this permanent butt. It's a good idea.

There are two types of ready-made leader—knotless and knotted. 'Knotless' or 'continuous taper' leaders taper steadily from butt to tip, much as a flyline does. On still water, especially if it happens to be calm as well, the knotless type is the more suitable—since even small knots can create little wakes behind them as line is retrieved. (Occasionally, indeed, trout mistake the knots for tiny insects and try to take them!) For really good presentation, however, the knotted type of leader is preferable. Its long thick butt, and the slight additional weight of the knots themselves, help it to carry into the wind and straighten out well. It is usually the best type for fishing a dry fly on rivers.

How long should the leader be? The normal length is 9 ft and this will usually serve you well. Longer leaders—up to perhaps 20 ft—can also be effective for certain purposes, sometimes to avoid scaring fish, sometimes to gain a little extra depth when fished with a floating line. But long leaders do need a good deal of skill to handle, especially in a wind. It is seldom if ever desirable, however, to have a leader *shorter* than 9 ft. (Even if you have a far shorter rod, the join between line and leader won't catch in the tip-ring while a fish is being played provided you've used a needle-knot or a cast connector.)

Braided-butt leaders

There are various forms and makes of braided-butt leader which can be bought. But they do not really vary very much. The braided butt itself is tapered, as of course it should be, and usually takes up half or rather more of the total leader's length. The braided portion can always be attached smoothly and neatly to the flyline, either with the aid of superglue or more often by means of a 'sleeve' which securely holds the line and braid together.

At the end of the braid will be ordinary nylon. Sometimes this steps down in two or three knotted stages to the leader-tip. Sometimes, however, one length of nylon only—an extra long leader-tip—leads directly from the braid. In each case, as the nylon becomes shorter, it can easily be replaced. Sometimes you should do this from the final knot (if the leader is one of those that step down) and sometimes from the end of the braid—with a nail knot or water knot, as shown in the next chapter.

One other method of replacement is to have a loop at the far end of the braid and then attach it to another loop at the near end of the nylon. This is the quickest and easiest way of replacing the nylon, but I myself think it hinders the leader, though only slightly, from turning over as smoothly as it might.

From some sources you can buy the braided butts alone, without any ordinary nylon attached. These butts are available in various lengths—typically 5 ft, 8 ft, and 12 ft. Then you finish off the leader yourself, stepping down or not as you find best, and with the nylon of your own choice. This is my own favourite alternative and I obtain 8 ft butts for all my dry-fly leaders.

A complete braided-butt leader costs about three times as much as an ordinary nylon leader. But to compensate for this, the braided portion should last the whole season, perhaps even longer. Your only additional cost will be replacement nylon.

Now for the advantages of braided-butt leaders, most particularly (though not exclusively) for dry-fly fishermen:

(a) Braid constitutes a far better continuation to your flyline than ordinary nylon. Ordinary nylon is usually almost five times stiffer than a flyline—which is patently a disadvantage both for smooth transmission of energy and for a good turnover. (Yet we didn't do so badly with the old leaders, did we?) Braid is as supple as a flyline, in fact a little more so.

(b) The braid portion of a braided-butt leader can therefore in effect be regarded as a flyline continuation. The genuine leader really only starts beyond it. This means that a braided-butt leader of considerable length can be cast just as easily as a far shorter leader made entirely of ordinary nylon. (The length I myself braided-butt leaders with which I now fish a dry fly on rivers are 13 to 14 ft long.) A long leader helps one to cast any given distance with less effort.

(c) The suppleness of braid enables it to turn over not only more smoothly than nylon, but also with a narrower loop. This is a considerable help both for distance-casting and casting into a wind. Yet it will not harm presentation, since the nylon at the end will still turn over gracefully and slowly.

(d) When you cast with a braided-butt leader, the improved transmission of energy allows you to use a very long piece of fine nylon as a leader-tip. The advantage here is obvious—a trout will see more thin nylon (if he sees it at all) and less thick nylon. The leader-tip on an ordinary knotted nylon leader is seldom more than 21 inches long. With a braided-butt leader it will be twice this length at the very least, and usually even longer.

(e) The combination of all the advantages above makes for greatly improved presentation. When you first use a braided-butt leader, you may find you have to slow down your casting just a little—because of its extra length. But then you are almost bound to be very pleased (if not downright conceited) about the consistency with which you can deliver your fly with maximum accuracy and delicacy.

(f) Braid has far more 'yield' than solid nylon. In other words it is more elastic. This allows it to cushion any sudden pull from a trout and you may be able to use a finer leader-tip as a result. Braid also has no memory (to quote fishing-tackle jargon) and never needs to be straightened out when it is first drawn from the reel.

Three types of braid

Braided-butt leaders can be bought with any of three possible types of braid.

(1) *Floating braid*. This is lighter than water, floats very well without any special treatment and is naturally ideal for the dry fly.

(2) *Intermediate braid*. This will float all day if greased. Without any grease it will sink a little below the surface.

(3) *Sinking braid*. This will sink faster and deeper than intermediate braid and can be of value in several forms of subsurface fishing. Solid nylon, for instance, is usually comparatively buoyant. So when it is attached directly to a sinking line, it may well lift the fly above the level of the line-tip. A braided-butt leader with sinking braid will help to keep the fly down. And again, when sinking braid is attached to a floating line, it will in effect transform it into a sink-tip line. It is often used for this purpose by salmon fishermen as well as others.

All the rest

There are of course a myriad other items of fishing tackle which you can buy. But in this chapter I've felt it best to deal with the essential items in some depth, rather than giving a more superficial description for all the luxuries and impedimenta which are such a temptation for all fishermen. There's one other essential item, of course—and that's a good selection of flies. All the more important dry flies, however, have been dealt with in earlier chapters. The list of further necessities isn't very long. It will probably include:

(a) *A landing net*. A net with a rigid frame—either round or oval—is the simplest and most efficient in use. Nets with collapsible triangular frames tend to let you down by getting in a tangle when you need them most. But they do have the advantage of being more compact to pack or carry around. For salmon fishing, you may need a large portable net or tailer.

(b) A pair of *thigh-waders*—or perhaps chest-waders if you fish for salmon in large rivers. Cleated rubber soles are adequate for most still waters, and also for rivers with a silt or gravel bed. But for the sake of safety choose felt or studded soles if you are wading in fast rocky streams.

(c) If you use a dry fly, you will need plenty of good *floatant* to make sure that the fly stays buoyant. There are a great many brands—so seek the advice of a good tackle dealer.

And that's that. Almost everything else is either non-essential or extremely easy to improvise. A flybox, for instance, is important for keeping flies in—but you can make one from any suitable container by lining it with ethafoam. A fishing waistcoat and/or bag is important too—but in a crisis an old haversack will serve instead.

You may well end up, like most of us, with too much tackle. But there's no need to *start* with too much.

CAUTIONARY FOOTNOTE

Good tackle is no substitute at all for skill or knowledge or experience. The right tackle helps a little, but no more. Fish never get caught by tackle. They get caught by fishermen.

CHAPTER 14

The Best Knots

Knots, like so many other things in fishing, should be demonstrated rather than written about. Once you have seen someone tie a particular knot, and watched where his fingers and thumbs go in the process, the knot seems far easier than it ever does on paper.

But the diagrams below and overleaf may help. They represent all the most useful knots for dry-fly fishing.

FIGURE OF EIGHT KNOT
For joining line to loop of leader

Pull tight

HALF BLOOD KNOT
The easiest knot for attaching fly to leader

Moisten, pull tight and cut off loose end

DOUBLE TURLE KNOT

A slightly better fly-to-leader knot—particularly useful when nylon is far finer than the eye of hook.

 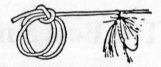

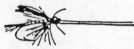

Pass fly through loops
draw tight and
cut off loose end.

FOUR-TURN (OR DOUBLE) BLOOD KNOT

For joining lengths of nylon.

Moisten, draw tight and cut off loose ends.

NEEDLE KNOT

The neatest knot for attaching flyline to leader, or rear of flyline to nylon backing.

Pierce line-tip with needle or large pin for about ¼". Point end of nylon with scissors or razor-blade and thread through.

Gently pull both ends of nylon so that coils lie tidily, but not too tightly around line and tubing.

Lay some hollow PVC tubing alongside line. Wind butt of leader 4 or 5 times round both line and tubing working from front to rear. Then thread butt of leader through tubing.

Slide tubing out beyond leader-butt. Then pull both ends of nylon till knot is tight around line. Snip off loose end of nylon.

NB. The Needle knot can be tied without the use of tubing, but tubing makes it far easier. The tubing should be around ½" in length and of fairly fine diameter. (The tube of a salmon fly will serve instead.)

SURGEON'S KNOT (OR WATER KNOT)
A strong and convenient knot for joining nylon, or for joining tippet to remainder of leader.

LEADER   TIPPET

Lay tippet and end of leader alongside each other, with rather more overlap than can be illustrated here.

Form simple overhand knot, using both strands of nylon.

Take end of leader and entire tippet twice more through loop.

Moisten, draw tight and cut off unwanted ends.

GEORGE HARVEY KNOT
Little known in Britain but considered by many Americans to be by far the best fly-to-leader knot.

1. Thread fly as shown.

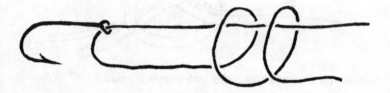

2. Make two loops as shown.

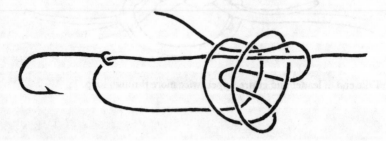

3. Take end of tippet *twice* through the two loops, as shown. Tighten by pulling on *both* ends of nylon. Finally, cut off loose end.

NAIL KNOT

Useful for attaching braided backing to fly line or for attaching nylon to a braided leader-butt.

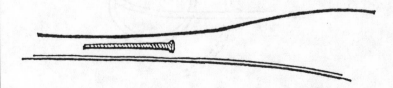

Instead of the nail shown here, a length of small diameter tubing (or body of tube fly) can be used. This simplifies tying.

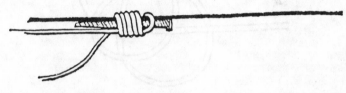

Wrap nylon (or backing) round 5 or 6 times.

Pass nylon back through coils (or tubing). Tighten by pulling both ends of nylon. Remove nail (or tubing) and tighten again.

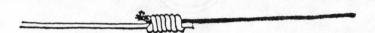

Cut off ends.

PERFECTION KNOT
For making loop at butt of leader

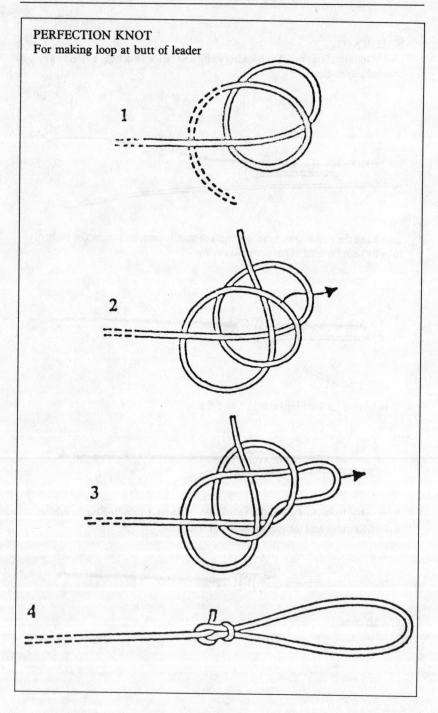

—◆◆◆ **Epilogue** ◆◆◆—

I should like to end this book with a plea—or rather, with some advice. I think it is good advice. But judge for yourself.

Fishing—not only dry-fly fishing but every other sort of fishing as well—depends on clean water. No fish, let alone a trout, will or can live in polluted water. And the law of the land, luckily, forbids anyone to pollute a river or lake, *for any reason whatsoever.* So if anyone pollutes your own fishing, or any fishing you legally lease, you have a perfect right to bring him into court, stop him doing it, and claim damages too.

But would you be able to afford it? The costs of such cases sometimes run into many thousands of pounds. My advice then, is this. Join the Anglers' Co-operative Association—the A.C.A. This organisation exists for the sole purpose of combating water pollution, and does so extremely successfully. It undertakes pollution cases on behalf of its members and indemnifies them against unaffordable costs. You can get full details by writing to the Director, A.C.A., Midland Bank Chambers, Westgate, Grantham, Lincs. NG31 6LE. Every new member will help not only to protect his own fishing, but also that of others, and also the interest of every man, woman or child who takes pleasure in rivers.

Another body which deserves your support as a trout fisherman is the Salmon and Trout Association. This organisation protects and furthers the interests of all game fishermen, by co-ordinating their views and wishes and representing these wherever the representation can be most effective, such as to Governments. The Association has done particularly useful work in opposing harmful schemes for water abstraction. If you don't know about the Association's work, please find out. Write for details to the Director, Salmon and Trout Association, Fishmongers' Hall, London EC4R 9EL.